ST. AUGUSTINE
ON FAITH AND WORKS

ANCIENT CHRISTIAN WRITERS

THE WORKS OF THE FATHERS IN TRANSLATION

EDITED BY

WALTER J. BURGHARDT

and

THOMAS COMERFORD LAWLER

Johannes Quasten, a founder of ACW, died on March 10, 1987. Needless to say, we miss him dearly. Father Quasten will be replaced soon on ACW by two scholars.

No. 48

St. Augustine
On Faith and Works

TRANSLATED AND ANNOTATED

BY

GREGORY J. LOMBARDO, C.S.C., S.T.D.

Professor of Theology
University of Portland

NEWMAN PRESS
New York, N.Y./Mahwah, N.J.

Library of Congress Cataloging-in-Publication Data

Augustine, Saint, Bishop of Hippo.
[De fide et operibus. English]
On faith and works / St. Augustine ; translated and annotated
by Gregory J. Lombardo.
p. cm. —(Ancient Christian writers ; no. 48)
Translation of: De fide et operibus.
Bibliography: p.
Includes indexes.
ISBN 0-8091-0406-7 : $16.95 (est.)
1. Faith—Early works to 1800. 2. Good works (Theology)—Early
works to 1800. I. Lombardo, Gregory J. II. Title. III. Series.
BR60.A35 no. 48
[BR65.A6567]
270 s—dc19
[234'.2] 88-1057
CIP

Published by Paulist Press
997 Macarthur Boulevard
Mahwah, New Jersey 07430

PRINTED AND BOUND IN THE UNITED STATES OF AMERICA

CONTENTS

Augustine, *Retractationes* 2.38: In the meantime I received from certain laymen who, however, were learned in the Scriptures, certain writings which so distinguished good works from Christian faith as to say that it was possible to obtain eternal life without the former but not without the latter. In answer to them I wrote a book which is entitled *On Faith and Works.* I show in this book not only how Christians ought to live, that is, those who have been regenerated by the grace of Christ, but also what kind of person we should admit to the bath of regeneration. This book begins as follows: "It is the opinion of some. . . ."

INTRODUCTION

Date of Composition and Purpose

In chapter 14.21 of the *De fide et operibus* St. Augustine mentions in passing that recently he published a work entitled *De spiritu et littera.*[1] We know that he finished this latter work towards the end of the year 412. Accordingly, he wrote the *De fide et operibus* early in the year 413. Moreover, this date is suggested by the fact that in his *Retractationes* Augustine places this work immediately after the *De spiritu et littera.*[2]

Augustine himself tells us why he wrote this work. Certain laymen, he says, had sent him some writings[3] to be examined. These writings taught that good works were not necessary to obtain eternal life, that faith alone was sufficient for salvation.[4] If a man had the faith and was baptized, he would be saved. Consequently, every man without exception should be admitted to baptism, no matter how evil his life, and even though he had no intention of changing for the better. Moreover, the instructions given to candidates for baptism should consist only in dogmatic truths, that is, only in those truths which one must believe as distinguished from those which one must put into practice.[5] This, in short, is the error which Augustine undertakes to refute in this book.

In his refutation Augustine points out in the first place that the Church is a mixed society, a society of saints and sinners (2.3 ff.). There are bad in the Church as well as good, and the bad will exist in the Church along with the good until the end of the world. It seems strange that Augustine should begin with this argument, but obviously his purpose is to answer the objection on the part of his opponents that, since there are sinners in the Church, the Church should be willing to admit sinners into its fold. Then, too, it must be remembered that at the time he wrote this work his long fight with the Donatists was still very fresh in his mind.[6] Against the former he argues that, although the Scriptures have foretold that there will always be sinners in the Church, nevertheless this does not mean that the Church should relax its discipline in their regard. On the contrary, she must punish, rebuke, and correct, as did Moses, St. Paul, and our Lord before her (2.3 ff.). Furthermore, our Lord forbids her to give what is holy to dogs.[7] On the other hand, strict discipline does not mean that we must start troublesome schisms in the Church, by presuming, for example, that we can separate the good from the bad before the appointed time. If we cannot correct the evil members of the Church, then for the sake of peace and unity we must tolerate them.

Augustine then takes up the question of baptism (6.8 ff.). In his treatment of this problem he gives a fairly detailed description of the requirements and of the preparation which the early Church demanded of all candidates for baptism. He points out to his opponents that the Church does not confer baptism on anyone who is not willing to repent of his sins and to accept the obligations of the new faith. For this reason she does not admit to her ranks any person who is engaged in a practice or profession which is not in keeping with the Christian way of life.[8] He states that this has always been the custom of the Church and that this custom is based on the clear teaching of Scripture.

In Augustine's time there was what might be called a remote and an immediate preparation for baptism. Augustine speaks of both in his treatise, but it is with the latter that he is chiefly concerned. This preparation took place usually during Lent and consisted in a series of exercises and instructions which had for their purpose the purification of the candidate and the completion of his knowledge of the Christian life. The candidate at this stage was technically known as a *competens*.[9] As we pointed out above, there were some at this time who wished to do away with a part of this preparation, with that part, namely, which concerned the moral instruction of the candidate. But Augustine shows here very clearly the fallacy of such an opinion. He argues that, if the Church deems it good and necessary to instruct catechumens, then how much more necessary and salutary it is to instruct those who are immediately preparing to receive so holy a sacrament (6.8).

The third and final question which Augustine treats in his little book is that of faith and works. In the fifth century there were two major errors regarding justification: the Pelagian heresy, which said that justification depended solely on man's efforts, and the heresy of justification by faith alone,[10] which Augustine refutes here in the *De fide et operibus* (14.21), and which he describes in these words: "This is that opinion which says that they who live most evil and most disgraceful lives, even though they continue to live in this way, will be saved and will gain eternal life, as long as they believe in Christ and receive His sacraments" (27.49). The proponents of this opinion appealed especially to the Scriptures in support of their argument, not only to St. Paul (Rom. 3.8, 28; 5.20), but also to the Gospels, as, for example, where Christ praises the faith of the Canaanite woman (Mt. 15.28).

For the Bishop of Hippo, however, the only faith that justifies is that faith which is enlivened by charity. Many times throughout his discussion he states very clearly and emphatically that faith without works is dead and cannot save. He warns the faithful that they will endanger the salvation of their souls if they act on the false assurance that faith alone is sufficient for salvation, or that they need not perform good works in order to be saved (14.21). He brings forth numerous texts from Scripture, both from the epistles of the apostles and from the Gospels, to prove that good works must be joined to faith if one hopes to be saved. "It is evident," he says, in referring to those whom Christ will place on His left hand at the Last Judgment (Mt. 25.41), "that He rebukes them, not because they did not believe in Him, but because they did not perform good works. In fact, this is why He said that He will separate all who were united together by the same faith, in order that no one might think that faith alone, or a dead faith, that is, a faith without works, is sufficient for eternal life" (15.25).

Augustine shows that this is the teaching of both St. Paul and St. James.[11] When Paul says that the *law entered in that sin might abound. And where sin abounded, grace did more abound* (Rom. 5.20), he does not mean to say, as some have thought, that man should *do evil that there may come good* (Rom. 3.8), but rather that it was necessary that God give man grace so that he could keep the law (14.21).[12] Likewise, when he says that man is justified by faith and not by the observance of the law (Rom. 3.28), he is speaking here of works before justification, not of works after justification.[13] "For the works of the law are meritorious not before but after justification" (14.21). Moreover, St. Paul does not say that any faith in God is good but that faith is good which results in works of love.[14] As for that faith which is dead, he says that it profits nothing: *If I should have all faith, so that I could remove mountains, and have not charity, I am nothing* (14.21).[15] In this way Augustine proves from St. Paul the necessity of good works.

As regards St. James, Augustine says that he "is so opposed to those who think that faith can save without good works that he compares them to devils" (14.23).[16] According to Augustine, the apostles Peter, John, James, and Jude insisted very strongly in their epistles on the necessity of good works because there were some even at that time who misinterpreted the teaching of Paul in this matter. He points out that Peter in his second epistle (3.11–18) warns the faithful that, although there are in Paul some things hard to understand, nevertheless he has the same mind on the question of eternal salvation as have all the other apostles (14.22). Thus, not only does Augustine indicate here that there is no opposition between Paul and James and the other apostles, but he shows also that there is no contradiction in Paul himself.

Faith and Works in Augustine's Other Writings

The problem of faith and works is not confined to the *De fide et operibus* but is discussed by Augustine in many of his other writings. The doctrine that he expresses in these is in some instances more complete, but basically the same as that which he expresses here. He compares the teaching of Paul with that of James and points out that the one speaks of works before justification, the other of works after justification. To those who place their trust in faith alone James recommends the works of Abraham, whose faith Paul praised. Thus, faith and works must be joined to one another. Abraham was justified by faith, not by works, but good works certainly followed his faith. If anyone objects that Paul does not teach this, then let him consider well Galatians 5.6, 14 and Romans 13.10. It is not necessary to contrast James with Paul, but Paul with Paul himself. The Apostle emphasized justification by faith without the works of the law in order to deprive man of self-praise and of the thought that faith is obtained by works.[17]

The faith that is deserving of praise is that faith by which the just man lives (Rom. 1.17), that faith by which we believe in him who justifies the impious (Rom. 4.5), that faith which excludes boasting (Rom. 3.27), and finally it is that faith which is made efficacious by love (Gal. 5.6), by that love, namely, which we obtain through faith and through the Holy Spirit (Rom. 5.5).[18] Faith is not from works, but works come from faith.[19] Faith is the first work through which all the other works are obtained.[20]

Faith cannot be merited by works; otherwise justification, of which faith is the beginning, would depend upon good works. We are not justified by the law, nor by our own wills, but gratuitously. Yet justification does not happen without our wills. For although the will is proved weak by the law, nevertheless it can be healed by grace, and healed by grace it can fulfil the law. When the good will is prepared by God (*bona voluntas praeparatur a Deo*) and grace precedes faith, then man begins to believe. To believe (*credere*) is a part of faith, which, however, is not a dead faith but a faith accompanied by hope and love.[21]

Insofar as faith contributes towards justification, it can be said to merit justification,[22] that is, faith merits for us the grace of God by which we are justified. Grace precedes faith, and faith obtains the grace of justification. Augustine does not explain the inner connection between one grace and the other, between faith and justification. He merely indicates the effect of one upon the other, that is, the causal relation of one to the other. And he does not show either in regard to faith as a virtue of the soul or in regard to faith as an act how love proceeds from faith. He emphasizes that justification must be produced by and through faith but he rejects the *sola fides*, the *fides mortua*, since it was also rejected by Paul (1 Cor. 13.2; 1 Tim. 1.5; 2 Tim. 1.5; 3.8). He demands that faith which works through love (Gal. 5.6), but this love does not come directly from faith but is a consequence of that faith which is diffused in our hearts by the Holy Spirit (Rom. 5.5).[23]

Editions and Translations

The text used for the present translation is that of the Vienna Corpus 41 (1900) vii–xiv and 35–97, edited and revised by Joseph Zycha.

Translations consulted are the following:

Cornish, C. L., in *Seventeen Short Treatises of S. Augustine* (A Library of Fathers of the Holy Catholic Church 6, Oxford 1847) 37–84.

Barreau, M. H., in *Oeuvres complètes de saint Augustin* 21 (Librairie de Louis Vivès, Editeur, Paris 1869) 242–86.

Mitterer, S., in *Des heiligen Kirchenvaters Aurelius Augustinus ausgewählte praktische Schriften, homiletischen und katechetischen Inhalts* (Bibliothek der Kirchenväter 49, Munich 1925) 312–85.

Liguori, Sister Marie, in *Saint Augustine: Treatises on Marriage and Other Subjects* (The Fathers of the Church 27, New York 1955) 213–82.

Pegon, J., in *Oeuvres de saint Augustin* (Bibliothèque augustinienne 8, Paris 1951) 345–461.

Perl, Carl Johann, *Aurelius Augustinus, Drei Bücher über den Glauben* (Deutsche Augustinusausgabe, Paderborn 1968) 88–192.

Chapter 1

Exposition of false doctrines which Augustine will answer in this treatise.

1. It is the opinion of some that all men without distinction should be admitted to the bath of regeneration[1] which is in Christ Jesus, our Lord, and that they should be admitted even though they are unwilling to change an evil and shameful life, a life notorious for manifest crimes and disgraceful deeds, and even though they declare openly and publicly that they will continue therein. If, for example, anyone is associated with a prostitute,[2] he should not first be commanded to leave her, and then come and be baptized. But even though he remains with her, and says or even declares openly that he will remain with her, he should be admitted to baptism. He should not be hindered from becoming a member of Christ,[3] even though he persists in being a member of a prostitute. Afterwards he can be taught how evil this is, namely, after he has been baptized; then it can be explained to him that he ought to change his life for the better. For these men think that it is wrong and even absurd that one should first be taught how to live a Christian life and then be baptized. They think rather that the sacrament of baptism should come first; the teaching concerning morals and the life of a Christian should follow afterwards.

If the baptized person fulfils the obligations demanded of a Christian, he does well. If he does not—provided he keeps the faith, without which he would perish forever—no matter in what sin or impurity he remains, he will be saved, as it were, by fire;[4] as one who has built on the foundation, which is Christ, not gold, silver, and precious stones, but wood, hay straw,[5] that is, not just and chaste works but wicked and unchaste works.

2. It seems that these men were influenced to think in this way

by their feeling for those who are not admitted to baptism, namely, those men and women who divorced their wives and husbands and married other wives and husbands.[6] But these persons are not admitted, because the Lord Christ declares without any doubt that such marriages are not marriages but adulteries.[7] Thus, they could not deny that that is adultery which the Truth clearly affirms is adultery. Nevertheless, they were in favor of admitting to baptism those who they saw were in such a predicament that, if they were not admitted, they would prefer to live or even die without any sacrament rather than free themselves from the bond of adultery. They were so moved by the plight of these persons that they thought that not only they but all evildoers should be admitted to baptism, and that they should be admitted without demanding of them that they abandon, correct, or change their evil ways. It is their opinion that these persons will perish forever if they are not admitted to baptism. But if they are admitted, even though they continue in their sin, they will be saved by fire.

Chapter 2

The example of Moses and of the apostle Paul shows that the Church should not relax her discipline, and that obstinate sinners should be punished.

3. In answer to them I say in the first place: let no man interpret those passages of Holy Scripture which speak of the present or future existence of good and bad in the Church as meaning that the discipline or vigilance of the Church ought to be relaxed or dispensed with. To give them this meaning would show that a person was ignorant of Scripture and deceived by his own thinking. And in the case of Moses, the servant of God, although he was very patient with those of his people who mingled with foreigners, nevertheless he also punished many even with death.[8] Likewise, Phinees the priest put to death with the sword the adulterers whom he had caught in the act.[9] In these examples we have a sign that the same was to be done in the Church by means of excommunication and degradation, since the ex-

ternal sword was no longer to be used in the discipline of the Church.[10] And also the blessed apostle Paul, although he is very patient in the midst of false brethren,[11] and although he permits some who were incited by a diabolical envy to preach Christ,[12] yet he does not think that that man should be spared who had *his father's wife.*[13] In fact, he orders that, when the Church is gathered together, such a one should be delivered over to *Satan for the destruction of the flesh, that the spirit may be saved in the day of the Lord Jesus.*[14] What is more, Paul himself delivered others up to *Satan, that they may learn not to blaspheme.*[15] Neither did he say in vain: *I wrote to you in an epistle not to keep company with fornicators. I mean not with the fornicators of this world or with the covetous or the extortioners or the servers of idols; otherwise you must needs go out of this world. But now I have written to you not to keep company if any man that is named a brother be a fornicator or covetous or a server of idols or a railer or a drunkard or an extortioner: with such a one, not so much as to eat. For what have I to do to judge them that are without? Do not you judge them that are within? For them that are without, God will judge. Put away the evil one from among yourselves.*[16]

Some indeed understand the words *from among yourselves* to mean that each man ought to remove evil from himself, that is, let every man see to it that he himself is good. In whatever way these words are understood, whether as meaning that the wicked should be punished by the Church with excommunications, or that each man should remove evil from himself by reproving and correcting himself,[17] nevertheless what was said above is clear, namely, that no man should keep company with those brethren who are classified with the sinners spoken of above, that is, with notorious and public sinners.

Chapter 3

The apostle Paul and the Lord Himself admonish the punishment of wrongdoers, but in a spirit of brotherly love and when circumstances permit.

However, St. Paul shows with what spirit and charity this merciful severity is to be used.[18] And he shows this not only in that place where he says: *that the spirit may be saved in the day of the Lord Jesus,*[19] but also in that other place where he says: *If any man obey not our word by this epistle, note that man and do not keep company with him, that he may be ashamed. Yet do not esteem him as an enemy but admonish him as a brother.*[20]

4. And as regards our Lord Himself, He was certainly an extraordinary model of patience. He permitted a devil among His twelve apostles until the day of His passion. It was our Lord who said: *Suffer both to grow until the harvest, lest perhaps, in your desire to gather up the cockle, you root up the wheat also together with it.*[21] And it was our Lord who prophesied that those nets which were a figure of the Church would catch and bring to the shore, that is, even to the end of the world, good and bad fishes. And whatever else our Lord said concerning the mingling of good and bad, whether openly or in parables, yet, even so, He did not think that the discipline of the Church should be dispensed with. On the contrary, He recommended that it should be used when He said: *Take heed to yourselves. If your brother shall offend against you, go and rebuke him between you and him alone. If he shall hear you, you shall gain your brother. And if he will not hear you, take with you one or two more, that in the mouth of two or three witnesses every word may stand. And if he will not hear the Church, let him be to you as the heathen and publican.*[22] To this recommendation He added this grave warning: *Whatever you loose on earth shall be loosed also in heaven; and whatever you bind on earth shall be bound also in heaven.*[23] Furthermore, He forbids us to give what is holy to dogs.[24] In like manner the Apostle says: *Them that sin reprove before all, that the rest may have fear.*[25] In saying this, he does not contradict the Lord who says: *Rebuke him between you and him.* For both procedures must be followed,[26] according to the various maladies of those whom we have undertaken, surely not to destroy, but to correct and heal. Consequently, we must heal one person in this way, another in that. Likewise, there are reasons why we overlook and tolerate evil in the Church. Then again, there are reasons why we chastise, rebuke, refuse admittance, or remove from membership in the Church.

Chapter 4

An immoderate interpretation of true doctrine is often the occasion of false doctrine.

5. For men go astray when they do not keep to a middle course in their thinking, when they eagerly take up one line of thought and do not consider other statements of divine authority, statements which would keep them from going astray and would direct them in the way of truth and moderation. This is true not only of the matter at hand but of other matters also. Some persons, having considered only those passages of Scripture which prescribe the adoration of one God only, have thought that the Father, Son, and Holy Spirit are one and the same.[27] Others, on the other hand, suffering, as it were, from a different kind of disease, having fixed their attention on those passages which speak of the Trinity, and not being able to understand how there can be only one God, since the Father is not the Son, nor the Son the Father, nor the Holy Spirit either the Father or the Son, have thought that there is a difference also of nature in the three divine Persons.[28] Some, seeing how the Scriptures praise holy virginity, condemn marriage.[29] Others, on the contrary, reflecting on those passages which praise chaste marriages, put marriage on a par with virginity.[30] Some, in reading *It is good, brethren, not to eat flesh and not to drink wine*[31] and other similar statements, think therefore that the creature of God and certain foods are unclean.[32] Others, however, on reading the words *Every creature of God is good, and nothing to be rejected that is received with thanksgiving*,[33] have allowed themselves to fall into drunkenness and greed,[34] not having it in their power to free themselves from sin. On the contrary, they fall into as great or even greater sins.

6. Thus, in this matter also which we are now considering, there are some men who see in Scripture nothing else except those passages which admonish us to be strict, to rebuke the unruly, not to give what is holy to dogs,[35] to regard as a heathen any man who does not heed the Church,[36] to cut off from the body any member that gives scandal. Such persons only make trouble for the Church; they

try to separate the cockle from the wheat before the appointed time. But because of their blindness they themselves rather are separated from union with Christ. Here we may cite as an example the Donatist schism.[37] But first let it be understood that I am not addressing those who know that Caecilianus[38] was unjustly attacked and calumniated, and who nevertheless are ashamed to admit it. Rather, I am addressing the others and to them I say, even if these men had been in the wrong, that was no reason for you to leave the Church.[39] You should have been patient with them and should have stayed in the Church, especially since you could not in any way correct or segregate them. Some, on the other hand, endanger the peace of the Church by going to the other extreme. These know that good and bad are in the Church and that it has been revealed and foretold in Scripture; and these know too that one must be patient with the bad.—As for ourselves, such knowledge makes us all the more strong, so much so that, even though there are evil men in the Church, we do not on that account quit the Church or forsake our faith and charity.—These, however, think that the Church should abandon its discipline. They want her to be free from any obligation of this kind, but it is a freedom that is most perverse. They think that the Church should only say what should or should not be done, but what one actually does, that should not be any concern of hers.

Chapter 5

We must tolerate the bad in order to safeguard the peace and unity of the Church. Nevertheless, we must not relax the discipline of the Church.

7. As for ourselves, we think that the true doctrine is had in moderation. Consequently, we are to tolerate evil men in the Church when the peace of the Church is at stake; but when it is not at stake, then we are not to give to dogs that which is holy. When we discover, therefore, that there are evil men in the Church whom the Church cannot reform or restrain, no matter how they gained entrance, whether through negligence on the part of the rulers of the Church,

or because of some excusable necessity, or by concealing their real purpose and intention, then let us not be so presumptuous and so proud as to think that we must separate ourselves from them so as not to be corrupted by their wickedness, or that we must gather around us a following, as it were, of good and holy men. To act in this way is only to cut ourselves off from the Church under the pretence of segregating ourselves from the wicked. Let us rather call to mind those parables of Sacred Scripture and those passages or striking examples which reveal and foretell that the bad will exist in the Church along with the good even to the end of the world and to the Day of Judgment,[40] but which reveal also that the good, though they share the same sacraments with the bad, will not suffer harm from them on that account, provided they do not consent to their evil deeds.[41] However, when the rulers of the Church have the opportunity of curbing the wicked without endangering the peace of the Church, then let us not be indifferent, but let us be strict on ourselves. If we keep these things in mind, we can be sure of walking in the way of the Lord, which is the way of moderation, and with Him as our guide and teacher we will not become indifferent when we should be patient, nor too harsh in our zeal when we should be moderate.

Chapter 6

Baptism should be given only after instructions in faith and morals.

8. Now that we know what the true doctrine is, namely, that we ought to be moderate in dealing with evil men in the Church, let us return to the problem at hand. Let us see whether it is right to admit all men to baptism, whether or not we should be on our guard lest we give to dogs that which is holy,[42] and whether we should even go so far as to admit to so sacred a sacrament those who openly practice adultery and who profess that they will continue to do so. Certainly, these people would not be admitted to baptism if, during the few days preceding its reception, they declared that they would not keep themselves continent but would continue to have relations with

their true and lawful wives. For these few days before baptism are a sacred time, a time when the candidate, after having handed in his name, is prepared for baptism by fasting, abstinence, and exorcisms. During this time, therefore, he is not permitted relations with his wife, even though at other times he is allowed intercourse with her.[43] If a married man, then, is refused admittance to baptism for refusing to observe a custom, how can we say that an adulterer who refuses to change his evil life should be allowed to receive this sacrament?

9. They say, however, that a man should be baptized first and then, after baptism, he can be instructed in regard to morals and right living. This is fittingly done when a man is at the point of death. Then, after he has been taught in the fewest possible words all that he must believe,[44] he may receive the sacrament immediately, so that, if he should die, he may leave this life absolved from all his sins. But if a man in good health asks to be admitted to baptism, and he has the time to go for instructions, then what better time is there to teach him how to live a good, Christian life than when he is all anxious and eager to receive this most salutary sacrament?[45] Or have we become such strangers to ourselves that we no longer remember our own conversion and how anxious and eager we were to receive instructions?[46] For at one time we ourselves had sought admission to baptism and for that reason we also were once called *competentes.*[47] Then, too, there are new converts every year. Do we not see how zealous they are in attending the instructions, the exorcisms, the scrutinies,[48] and also how eager, how interested? If this is not the time to teach them morals that are worthy of a Christian and of this great sacrament which they are so desirous of receiving, then when is it? After baptism? This is what our opponents would like. In that case they would allow them to receive baptism without first demanding that they change their evil way of life, without demanding that they first put off the old man and then put on the new. Instead, they would advise just the opposite: first put on the new man, and after you have put on the new man, then put off the old. But this is not what the Apostle says. He says: *Put off the old man and put on the new.*[49] And the Lord says: *No man sews a new piece to an old garment and no man puts new wine into old wineskins.*[50] Moreover, for what other reason do we call them catechumens[51] and put them into this category for a certain time, except that they might learn what the faith is and

what kind of life is demanded of a Christian? Then, after they have proved themselves worthy, they may eat at the Lord's table and drink from His cup.[52] For *He who eats and drinks unworthily eats and drinks judgment to himself.*[53] If the Church thinks that it is good and necessary to give instructions to the catechumens, then certainly it is good and much more necessary and much more urgent to give instructions to the *competentes* who are immediately preparing to receive baptism.

Chapter 7

The opponents of Augustine cannot prove their assertions from the epistles of the apostles.

10. What if a single woman, they ask, marries in good faith a married man? As long as she remains in good faith, she is not an adulteress. But once she discovers that her husband has been married before, from then on she is an adulteress, if she consents to live with him as his wife. The same applies here in marriage as in the case of a possessor in good faith. A man is considered, and very justly so, a possessor in good faith as long as he does not know that what he possesses belongs to another. But once he knows that what he has belongs to another, and he does not return it to the rightful owner, then he is considered a possessor in bad faith and he is rightly called unjust. Let us not, then, be deceived by a false pity. Let us not feel that in correcting such evils we are destroying the bond of matrimony. We in particular should know better, for we dwell *in the city of our God, in His holy mountain*,[54] namely, the Church, which regards matrimony not only as a contract[55] but also as a sacrament.[56] Consequently, she does not allow a man to give his wife to another,[57] as Cato is said to have done in the days of the Roman Republic, and for this he was not in the least censured but was even praised.[58] There is no need now, however, to discuss this matter any further, for even our opponents do not dare to say that such an action is not sinful, or that it is not adultery, because they know that such a statement would be in open contradiction to the teaching of our Lord Himself and of

His holy Gospel. It is their opinion, nevertheless, that such persons should be allowed to receive baptism and to eat at the Lord's table, even though they openly refuse to give up their evil ways. Furthermore, they say that we should not at all reprove them for their evil conduct before they are baptized, but should admonish them after they are baptized that they should change their lives for the better. If, after they are baptized and instructed, they change their evil habits and lead good, Christian lives, they will be counted among the wheat; if they do not, they will be counted among the cockle. At any rate, it is evident that our opponents do not defend these crimes or act as if they were of small importance or nothing at all. For what Christian worthy of the name would regard adultery as a light sin or no sin at all?[59]

11. This procedure, namely, that of allowing these persons to be baptized first and instructed afterwards, with the hope that they will change their evil ways and lead a good, Christian life, this procedure, they say, is contained in the Holy Scriptures. According to them, this is what the apostles did, as can be proven from their epistles, for they find in these epistles evidence that the apostles instructed their hearers in doctrine first and in morals afterwards. On the basis of this evidence, therefore, they would have us understand that we are to make known only the rule of the faith[60] to those who are to be baptized, and only after they have been baptized are we to give them precepts of conduct in the hope that they will change their lives for the better. It is as if the apostles addressed certain epistles, in which they treat of doctrine only, to those who are to be baptized; whereas other epistles, in which they treat of morals, they addressed to those already baptized. It is certain, however, that the apostles addressed epistles to Christians already baptized. Why, then, do they in these epistles treat of matters that pertain to both faith and morals? What do our opponents say to this? Perhaps now they would say that we are not to give any instructions at all to those who are to be baptized, but to those already baptized we are to give instructions in both faith and morals. But if it is absurd to say this, then let them admit that the apostles treated of both in their epistles, that is, of faith and of morals. In general, the apostles first treated of faith and then of morals, but this was because they realized that a man must have the faith first before he can live a good, Christian life. For whatever mor-

ally good act a man may seem to perform, it is not a morally good act unless it is done out of devotion to God.[61] But even if some persons were so foolish and so ignorant as to think that the apostles addressed their epistles to catechumens, yet even these persons would admit that those who are not yet baptized should be instructed in the morals of the faith as well as in the doctrines of the faith. If they do not admit this, then they force us to say that the first portions of the epistles, in which portions the apostles treat of faith, are intended for catechumens, whereas the latter portions, in which they treat of Christian morals, are intended for the faithful. If this sounds very absurd, there is then no proof from the epistles of the apostles that we are to teach those who are to be baptized doctrine only, but the baptized, the precepts of Christian morality. It is foolish to try to prove this from the fact that the apostles in their epistles speak first of faith and then exhort the faithful to live good, Christian lives. Moreover, this procedure would be very impractical. The reason is that it is often necessary in our instructions to treat of faith and morals together,[62] and not only necessary but also very practical and wise. This is true whether we are instructing catechumens, or the faithful,[63] or those who are to be baptized, or those already baptized;[64] and it holds for any purpose that we might have in instructing them, whether to refreshen their memories, or to have them profess the faith, or to strengthen them in the faith. In conclusion, then, besides the passages from the epistles of Saints Peter and John, which our opponents cite in favor of their opinion, let them also add to these, if they so desire, passages from the epistles of Paul and of the other apostles. Let them say, if they will, that these also treated first of faith and then of morals in their epistles. As for ourselves, we have shown very clearly, if we are not mistaken, the fallacy of such an opinion.

CHAPTER 8

The first preaching (sermon) of St. Peter testifies to the necessity of penance and renunciation of the world for all who wish to be baptized.

12. Our opponents still insist, however, that the apostles spoke only of faith in Christ to those who are to be baptized. This, they say, is what Peter did when, as related in the Acts of the Apostles, he preached to a large number of people; and it is related that three thousand of those who heard him were baptized in one day. And when they had asked Peter: *What shall we do?*, he answered them: *Do penance and be baptized every one of you in the name of the Lord Jesus Christ for the remission of sins, and you shall receive the gift of the Holy Spirit.*[65] Why, then, do they not take notice of what was said, namely, *do penance?* For it is by repentance that we strip off the old man, so that, when we are baptized, we may be clothed with the new. But how can any person be sincerely repentant for his sins if he continues to commit adultery and other grievous sins which the lovers of this world are wont to commit?

13. They say, however, that Peter willed that they should repent only for their unbelief in Christ. What an assumption, to say the least! They presume that to *do penance* means here repentance for unbelief only. But this is not the kind of repentance which the Gospels preach, for they tell us that we must put off the old man and put on the new. Nor is it the kind which St. Paul speaks of when he says: *He that stole, let him now steal no more.*[66] In this statement and in others also St. Paul explains what is meant by putting off the old man and putting on the new. Moreover, if they were attentive to what St. Peter says, they would understand what he means. For when he says: *Do penance and be baptized every one of you in the name of the Lord Jesus Christ for the remission of sins, and you shall receive the gift of the Holy Spirit. For to us is this promise and to our children and to all that are far off, whomsoever the Lord our God shall call*, the author of the book immediately adds: *And with many other words he bore witness saying: Save yourselves from this wicked world. They indeed listened very eagerly and accepted his words and believed and*

were baptized; and there were added on that day three thousand souls.[67] Who cannot perceive here that in these *many other words*—which words the author passes over for the sake of brevity—Peter urged his listeners to save themselves from this wicked world, especially since it is briefly mentioned that this was his purpose in speaking many words? In fact, the sum and substance of his sermon is contained in the words *Save yourselves from this wicked world*, and in order that his listeners might do this, Peter bore witness to them in many words. We have in these words a condemnation of dead works, which the lovers of this world impiously perform, and a recommendation of a virtuous life for those to hold and follow who renounce this wicked world. Now, then, let our opponents try to affirm, if they will, that that man renounces this wicked world who merely believes in Christ and who continues to commit whatever sins he pleases, even to the extent of living in public adultery. But if it is wrong to say this, then those who are to be baptized should hear not only what they are to believe but also how they are to renounce this wicked world. For it is at this time especially, when they are about to be baptized, that they should be taught how Christians ought to live.[68]

CHAPTER 9

The example of the eunuch baptized by Philip does not prove that all that is needed to receive baptism is merely to profess the divinity of Christ.

14. They say, however, that the eunuch whom St. Philip baptized did not say anything more than *I believe that Jesus Christ is the Son of God*,[69] and having made this profession of faith, he was immediately baptized. Is it, then, their wish that men should make no more profession of faith than this, and then be immediately baptized? What about the other truths of the faith, those, namely, concerning the Holy Spirit, the Church, the forgiveness of sins, the resurrection of the dead, and, finally, those concerning the Lord Jesus Himself? Is nothing to be said or believed concerning these? Is nothing to be

said or believed about the Lord except that He is the Son of God? Nothing about His incarnate birth from a virgin, His passion, His death on the cross, His burial, His resurrection on the third day, His ascension, and His place at the right hand of the Father? If all that the eunuch had to say was *I believe that Jesus Christ is the Son of God* in order that he be baptized immediately and allowed to go his way, why then do we not follow suit? Why do we not act in like manner and do away with all these other truths which must be professed by everyone who is baptized,[70] even when time is pressing, and even though the subject cannot commit them to memory?[71] If the Scriptures have been silent and have left it to us to understand that Philip did all that was necessary in baptizing the eunuch, and if they mean for us to understand, when they say *Philip baptized him*, that everything was done which we know from tradition must be done—for the Scriptures, for the sake of brevity, do not mention everything that must be done—in like manner, when they say that Philip preached to the eunuch about the Lord Jesus, we must not at all doubt that in his preaching[72] he talked about the manner of life one should lead and the morals one should have who believes in the Lord Jesus. This is to preach Christ: to say not only what one must believe about Christ but also how one must live who wishes to be joined to the body of Christ;[73] to say, in fact, everything that one must believe about Christ, not only whose Son He is, from whom He takes His divinity, from whom His humanity, what things He has suffered and why, what His resurrection means to us, what is the gift of the Spirit[74] which He has promised and given to believers, but also what kind of members, of whom He is the head,[75] He desires, He forms, loves, sets free, and leads to eternal life and glory. When all this is said, whether at times more fully and profusely, or at times more briefly and concisely, then is Christ preached, and still in all, nothing is left out, neither anything that pertains to faith nor anything pertaining to morals.

Chapter 10

The words of the apostle Paul, who knows only Christ crucified, contain the whole teaching of Christ, a doctrine, namely, of crucifixion and of love.

15. What we have been saying above applies also to that saying of the apostle Paul, namely, *I have said that I know nothing among you except Jesus Christ and Him crucified.*[76] I mention this saying in particular because our opponents quote it in their favor. They say that St. Paul means here—as if he could not have meant anything else—that his hearers should first of all profess the faith and then, after they have been baptized, they may be taught all that pertains to moral living. This, they say, was enough and more than enough for the apostle, who, we must remember, said to these same people that, even though they had *many instructors in Christ*, yet they have not had *many fathers*, because *in Christ Jesus, by the gospel*, he himself had begotten them.[77] If he who begot them through the gospel, although he gives thanks that he baptized none of them except Crispus, Gaius, and the household of Stephanas,[78] did not teach them anything more than Christ crucified, what then would our opponents answer if someone should say to them: How is it possible that they who were begotten through the gospel never heard of the resurrection of Christ? If St. Paul had taught them nothing except Christ crucified, how then do they explain that he says to them: *For I delivered unto you first of all that Christ died according to the Scriptures, and that He was buried, and that He arose the third day, according to the Scriptures?*[79] However, if this is not the way they understand this saying of St. Paul, but maintain rather that in preaching Christ crucified he preached to them the resurrection also, since the two are intimately connected, then let them also understand that in Christ crucified men understand many things, and this in particular, namely, that *Our old man is crucified with Him, that the body of sin may be made void, to the end that we may serve sin no longer.*[80] Wherefore St. Paul says of himself: *But God forbid that I should glory, save in the cross of our Lord Jesus Christ, by whom the world is crucified to me, and I to the world.*[81] Let them

take heed, then, and understand what we mean by Christ crucified. Let them understand that with him we are crucified to the world, that is, we are crucified to every evil desire. And for this reason they who are formed by the cross cannot be permitted to live in public adultery. This is the mind also of the apostle Peter, who, when speaking of the mystery of the cross, that is, of the passion of Christ, urges those who are sanctified by the cross to sin no more. This is what he says: *Christ therefore having suffered in the flesh, be you also armed with the same thought; for he who is dead in the flesh sins no more, that now he may live the rest of his time in the flesh, not after the desires of men but according to the will of the Lord God.*[82] And in the words that follow these, Peter shows that that man belongs to Christ crucified, that is, to Christ who has suffered in the flesh, who in his own body has crucified the desires of the flesh and lives a good life according to the gospel.

16. Our opponents also quote in favor of their opinion those two commandments on which, as the Lord says, the whole law and the prophets depend, namely: *You shall love the Lord your God with your whole heart and with your whole soul and with your whole mind. And the second is like to this: you shall love your neighbor as yourself.*[83] The first commandment, which obliges us to love God, pertains, they say, to those who are preparing for baptism; the second, which prescribes our obligations to our fellow men, to those already baptized. They forget, however, that it is written: *If you do not love your brother whom you see, how can you love God whom you do not see?*[84] They forget also that other saying of John, namely, *If any man love the world, the charity of the Father is not in him.*[85] For what else is sin if not the love of this world? It is evident that the first commandment, even if it should pertain only to those who are preparing for baptism, cannot in any way be observed without observing the laws of morality. But I do not wish to dwell on this subject any longer. For it should be evident to anyone who carefully considers these two commandments that they are so intimately connected with one another that it is impossible for a man to love God and not love his neighbor, or to love his neighbor and not love God. However, as regards these two commandments, what we have said about them here suffices for the subject which we are considering.

CHAPTER 11

Augustine answers his opponents' false interpretation of the passage through the Red Sea and of the giving of the law at Sinai.

17. But our opponents have still another objection. The people of Israel, they say, were first led through the Red Sea, which is a figure of baptism,[86] and then they were given the law by which they were to live. Since this was the case with the Israelites, why then do we demand that our catechumens learn the creed and recite it back to us?[87] Nothing of the kind was demanded of the Israelites whom God delivered from the Egyptians by leading them through the Red Sea. Our opponents say, and they are right, that their preparation for baptism, that is, before passing through the Red Sea, were the religious ceremonies of sprinkling their doorposts with the blood of the lamb and of eating the unleavened bread of sincerity and truth.[88] But if they understand correctly the significance of these religious ceremonies of the Israelites, why do they not also understand that their departure from Egypt signifies a renouncement of sin, which renouncement they make who are preparing to receive baptism? This is what Peter means when he says: *Do penance and be baptized every one of you in the name of our Lord Jesus Christ.*[89] It is as if he said, depart from Egypt and pass through the Red Sea. Likewise, in the Epistle to the Hebrews,[90] where mention is made of the essential doctrines required of the catechumens, one of these mentioned is repentance from dead works. The passage reads thus: *Wherefore, leaving the word of the beginning of Christ, let us look forward to the full accomplishment, not laying again the foundation of penance from dead works and of faith in God, of the doctrine of baptism, of the imposition of hands, also of the resurrection of the dead and of the eternal judgment.*[91] Thus, it is clear from Scripture that all these fundamental doctrines are a part of the instructions given to converts. But what, I ask, is repentance from dead works if not from those works which we must renounce if we wish to live? And if adultery and fornication are not dead works, then what is? It is not enough, therefore, to promise to re-

nounce such works unless all past sins, which, as it were, pursue after us, are washed away by the waters of baptism, just as it was not enough for the Israelites to depart from Egypt if the enemy who pursued them had not perished in the waves of the sea, of that same sea which rolled back its waters for the people of God to pass through and escape. How, then, can anyone who declares that he will not renounce the sin of adultery, how can such a one pass through the Red Sea, since as yet he refuses to depart from Egypt? Furthermore, our opponents seem to forget that in the law, which the Israelites received after they crossed the Red Sea, the first commandment is: *You shall not have other gods besides me. You shall not make idols for yourself nor any image, whether of anything in the heavens above or of anything on the earth below, or of anything in the waters under the earth. You shall not adore them and neither shall you serve them,*[92] and the rest which belongs to this commandment. Let them affirm, therefore, if they will, even in contradiction to their former assertion, that we are to speak of the worship of the one God and of renouncing idolatry not to those preparing for baptism but to those already baptized. And let them no longer say that to converts preparing for baptism we need speak only of faith in God, and that only after they have been baptized should we speak to them of moral obligations, or, in other words, of the second commandment, which obliges us to love our neighbor. For both commandments are contained in the law, in that law,[93] namely, which the people of Israel received after they had crossed the Red Sea, that is, to speak in a figurative sense, after they were baptized. Nor was there any division of the law, such as, for example, before crossing the sea the people were instructed to renounce idolatry, and after having crossed they were told to honor father and mother, not to commit adultery, not to kill,[94] and everything else which makes for good and just living between men.

CHAPTER 12

A case against the opponents.

18. Let us suppose that a man comes and asks to be baptized, but says that he will not give up sacrificing to idols unless, perhaps, at some future time, if he so wills. This man is not only a worshiper of idols but also a priest of some abominable cult. Nevertheless, he asks to be baptized immediately and to become the temple of the living God. I ask our opponents if they think that such a person should be admitted even as a catechumen.[95] Most assuredly they will say that he should not be admitted, and I do not at all doubt that they are sincere. Nevertheless, I ask them to show from Scripture why he should be refused admittance, even though he implores and says: I have come to know and worship Christ crucified; I believe that Jesus Christ is the Son of God. Do not put me off any longer and do not require anything more of me. The Apostle did not require anything more of those whom he begot through the gospel than that they know Christ crucified. When the eunuch said that he believed that Jesus Christ is the Son of God, Philip did not delay but baptized him immediately. Why, then, do you forbid me to worship idols and keep me from receiving the sacrament of Christ[96] until I have given up such a practice? I have learned it from childhood and I am compelled to it by force of habit. I will give it up as soon as I can, as soon as it is convenient to do so. But if I do not, still in all I do not want to die without the sacrament of Christ, lest God demand my soul from your hands.

How would they answer this man? Do they think he should be admitted? No, I do not at all believe that they are come to this. Nevertheless, what will they answer him? What will they answer him if he says that nothing should be said to him about renouncing idolatry—at any rate, nothing should be said before baptism; the people of Israel heard nothing about it before they crossed the Red Sea, for they did not receive the law until after their escape from Egypt. Surely they will say to him: you become the temple of God when you receive baptism, and, says the Apostle, *What agreement has the temple of God with idols?*[97] Why, then, do they not see that they ought to say in like manner: you become a member of Christ when you receive baptism; but the members of Christ cannot be the members of a prostitute?[98] For the Apostle says this too. And in another place he says: *Do not err; neither fornicators nor idolaters*, and the others whom he mentions here, *shall possess the kingdom of God.*[99] If we do not allow idolaters to be baptized, why do we allow fornicators, since the Apostle says to them as well as to other evildoers: *And such some of you were, but you are washed, but you are sanctified, but you are justified in the name of the Lord Jesus Christ and the Spirit of our God?*[100] Since I have the obligation to refuse baptism to both, the idolater and the fornicator, why then do I refuse the one and not the other? Does not the Apostle say to the one as well as to the other: *And such were some of you, but you have been washed?* But the reason why our opponents think that the one may be admitted, but not the other, is this: they think that these persons are saved, although by fire, if they believe in Christ and receive His sacrament, that is, if they are baptized.[101] They are saved, so they think, even though they do not correct their evil ways but go on living evil lives. But as regards this question, we shall soon see, with God's help, what we are to think according to the Scriptures.

Chapter 13

An argument from John the Baptist and from Christ.

19. At present, however, I am still interested in the question of instructions. Our opponents are of the opinion that we should not instruct converts in Christian morals until after they are baptized, and that before they are baptized we should not teach them anything except what they must believe. But if this were the case, besides the many arguments against it which we have already mentioned, another is that John the Baptist would not have said to those who came to him to be baptized: *You brood of vipers, who has showed you to flee from the wrath to come? Bring forth, therefore, fruit worthy of penance,*[102] and so forth. Certainly John is speaking here not of matters pertaining to

faith but of good works. Likewise, to the soldiers who asked him: *What shall we do?*, he did not say: believe in the meantime and be baptized; afterwards you will learn what you are to do. Rather, he spoke to them and admonished them beforehand in order that, as the forerunner of the Lord, he might prepare them to receive Him into their hearts. And this is what he said to them: *Do violence to no man, neither calumniate any man, and be content with your pay.*[103] And again, when the publicans asked him what they should do, he said to them: *Exact no more than what has been appointed you.*[104] The Evangelist, in making a brief mention of these instructions[105]—we should not expect him to mention everything—has given sufficient evidence that we are to teach those preparing for baptism the principles of Christian morality. But let us suppose that these men had said to John: we will not bring forth fruit befitting repentance, we will accuse falsely, we will do violence, we will exact what is not owed to us, and that, nevertheless, John had baptized them. Still we could not say, in regard to instructing converts—for this is the question we are now considering—that the time before baptism is not the proper time to teach them to live a good, Christian life.

20. Let them call to mind—to mention only one more argument—what the Lord Himself said to the rich man who asked Him what he should do to obtain eternal life. *If you will enter into life*, said the Lord, *keep the commandments.* The rich man said to him: *Which?* The Lord then gave him the commandments of the law: *You shall do no murder, you shall not commit adultery*, and the rest. And when the rich man said that he had observed them from the beginning, the Lord said to him that, if he wanted to be perfect, he should sell all that he had and give it in alms to the poor, so that he might have treasure in heaven, and that he should follow Him.[106] It should be evident to our opponents that He did not tell him to believe and be baptized—according to them a man would not have to do any more than this to obtain eternal life. On the contrary, He gave him precepts of morality which, certainly, one cannot observe unless he has faith also. For we do not want anyone to think that, because the Lord says nothing here about faith, we say and maintain therefore that it is not necessary to instruct a person who desires to obtain eternal life in anything except morals. Both are necessary, morals and faith, for they are mutually connected, as I said before.[107] A man who does not

love God does not love his neighbor; and he who does not love his neighbor does not love God. This is why the Scriptures sometimes speak of one and not of the other, either of faith or of morals, instead of both together, so that we might perceive from this procedure that the one cannot exist apart from the other. For he who believes in God ought to do what God commands; likewise, he who does what God commands ought to believe in God.

Chapter 14

The question of faith and works: faith without works is dead.

21. Let us now consider the question of faith. In the first place, we feel that we should advise the faithful that they would endanger the salvation of their souls if they acted on the false assurance that faith alone is sufficient for salvation or that they need not perform good works in order to be saved. This, in fact, is what some had thought even in the time of the apostles. For at that time there were some who did not understand certain rather obscure passages of St. Paul, and who thought therefore that he had said: *Let us do evil that there may come good.*[108] They thought that this was what St. Paul meant when he said: *The law entered in that sin might abound. And where sin abounded, grace did more abound.*[109] But what St. Paul means here is this: when man received the law, he presumed too much on his own strength. He was too proud to ask God's help, as he should have done, that he might overcome his evil desires. The result was that his sins were now more and greater because of the law which he did not observe. When he realized his guilt, he turned to the faith for pardon and for *help from the Lord, who made heaven and earth.*[110] Thus it was necessary that the Holy Spirit fill his heart with love,[111] in order that he might overcome his evil desires and perform out of love for God whatever God commanded him.[112] This is what St. Paul means, and this too is what the Psalmist means when he says: *Their infirmities were multiplied; afterwards they made haste.*[113]

When St. Paul says, therefore, that man is justified by faith and not by the observance of the law,[114] he does not mean that good works are not necessary or that it is enough to receive and to profess the faith and no more. What he means rather and what he wants us to understand is that man can be justified by faith, even though he has not previously performed any works of the law. For the works of the law are meritorious not before but after justification.[115] But there is no need to discuss this matter any further, especially since I have treated of it at length in another book entitled *On the Letter and the Spirit*.[116]

As we said above, this opinion originated in the time of the apostles, and that is why we find some of them, for example, Peter, John, James, and Jude, writing against it in their epistles and asserting very strongly that faith is no good without works. And as regards Paul himself, he does not say that any faith in God is good, but he says clearly that that faith is good and in conformity with the teaching of the gospel which results in works of love: *and faith*, he says, *that worketh by charity*.[117] As for that faith which some think is sufficient for salvation, he says that it profits nothing: *If I should have all faith, so that I could remove mountains, and have not charity, I am nothing*.[118] On the other hand, where faith is joined to charity, there without doubt you will find a good life, for *charity is the fulfilment of the law*.[119]

22. We can see, then, why St. Peter in his second epistle urges the faithful to live good and holy lives, reminding them that this world will pass away and that they are to look for new heavens and a new earth which the just will inhabit, and that, consequently, they ought to live so as to be worthy of such a dwelling place. He was aware of the fact that certain unrighteous men had interpreted certain rather obscure passages of St. Paul to mean that they did not have to lead a good life, since they were assured of salvation as long as they had the faith. He warns them that, although there are certain passages in the epistles of St. Paul which are hard to understand—which passages some have misinterpreted, as they have other passages of Sacred Scripture, but to their own ruin—nevertheless, St. Paul has the same mind on the question of eternal salvation as have all the other apostles, namely, that eternal salvation will not be given except to those who lead a good life. Here are St. Peter's own words: *Seeing, then, that all these things are to pass away, what manner of people ought you to be in holy conversation and godliness? Looking for and hasting unto the coming of the day of the Lord, by which the heavens being on fire shall be*

dissolved and the elements shall melt with the burning heat. But we look for new heavens and a new earth according to His promises, in which justice dwells. Wherefore, dearly beloved, waiting for these things, be diligent that you may be found before Him unspotted and blameless in peace. And account the long-suffering of our Lord salvation; as also our most dear brother Paul, according to the wisdom given him, has written to you. As also in all his epistles, speaking in them of these things; in which are certain things hard to be understood, which the unlearned and unstable wrest, as they do also the other Scriptures, to their own destruction. You therefore, most beloved, knowing these things before, take heed lest, being led aside by the error of unhappy men, you fall from your own steadfastness. But grow in grace and in the knowledge of our Lord and Savior Jesus Christ. To Him be glory both now and unto the day of eternity.[120]

23. St. James, moreover, is so opposed to those who think that faith can save without good works that he compares them to devils.[121] *You believe*, he says, *that there is one God? You do well; the devils also believe and tremble.*[122] Could he have said anything more concise, more true, more forceful, since, as we read in the Gospel, this is what the devils professed when they acknowledged that Christ is the Son of God? But Christ rebuked the devils, while, on the contrary, he praised St. Peter for making the same profession.[123] St. James says also: *What shall it profit, my brethren, if a man say he has faith, but has not works? Shall faith be able to save him?*[124] And in another place he says that *faith without works is dead.*[125] See, then, what a great mistake they make who think that they can be saved by a faith that is dead!

Chapter 15

Augustine reviews a false interpretation of 1 Cor. 3.11–15.

24. It is necessary, therefore, that we examine carefully and that we try to understand what St. Paul means in that difficult passage

where he says: *For other foundation no man can lay but that which is laid, which is Christ Jesus. Now if any man build upon the foundation gold, silver, precious stones, wood, hay stubble, every man's work shall be manifest. For the day shall declare it, because it shall be revealed in fire, and the fire shall try every man's work of what sort it is. If any man's work abide, which he has built thereupon, he shall receive a reward; but if any man's work burn, he shall suffer loss, but he himself shall be saved, yet so as by fire.*[126] Some interpret this passage to mean that they who have faith in Christ and also perform good works build upon this foundation gold, silver, and precious stones; but they who have the same faith and do not perform good works build upon it wood, hay, and stubble. This is the reason why they think that such persons can be purified by a certain kind of fire, a fire that causes suffering, but by means of which they will be able to obtain salvation, since they have built upon the foundation.[127]

25. If this is what this passage means, then those who are of this opinion deserve to be praised for their charity, that is, for trying to have everyone without distinction admitted to baptism, not only those who, contrary to the command of the Lord, live in adultery, but prostitutes also. If this is their reason for admitting everyone to baptism, then I do not see why these last should not be admitted also, despite the fact that they intend to continue in this most disgraceful practice, and despite the fact that never in any church, not even in the most lax, has it been the custom to admit them to baptism unless they first abandoned their evil profession.[128] For who would not prefer to see them build on the foundation even wood, hay, and stubble and be saved by fire, even if they have to suffer a long time, rather than see them perish forever?

But if this interpretation is correct, then all the following statements of Scripture are false, though they are clear and explicit in their meaning. For example, this statement of St. Paul: *If I should have all faith, so that I could remove mountains, and have not charity, I am nothing.*[129] And this of St. James: *What shall it profit, my brethren, if a man say he has faith, but has not works? Shall faith be able to save him?*[130] This likewise: *Do not err; neither fornicators, nor idolaters, nor adulterers, nor the effeminate, nor liers with mankind, nor thieves, nor covetous, nor drunkards, nor railers, nor extortioners shall possess the kingdom of God.*[131] And this: *The works of the flesh are manifest, which are fornications, unclean-*

nesses, luxury, idolatry, witchcrafts, enmities, contentions, emulations, hatreds, dissensions, heresies, envies, drunkenness, revelings, and such like. Of the which I foretell you, as I have foretold you, that they who do such things shall not possess the kingdom of God.[132] All these, then, are false. For if all one has to do is believe and be baptized, though he continues to commit such sins as these, he will be saved by fire. Consequently, those already baptized in Christ, if they commit these sins, they too will possess the kingdom of God.

Moreover, if this opinion is true, then it has been said in vain: *Such some of you were, but you are washed,*[133] since even after they have been washed, they are such. In like manner, St. Peter spoke in vain when he said: *Thus you also in a like manner baptism does save, not the putting away of the filth of the flesh, but the examination of a good conscience.*[134] For a person may be saved by baptism, even though his conscience is burdened with many sins and offenses for which he is not sorry. As long as he builds on the foundation which is laid for him in baptism, he will be saved, although by fire. But then I do not see why the Lord said: *If you will enter into life, keep the commandments,*[135] or why, after He had said this, He listed those which one must keep in order to live a good life,[136] if one can obtain eternal life without keeping the commandments, by faith alone, which *without works is dead.*[137] And then, too, how will the Lord be able to say to those whom He will place on His left hand: *Go you into everlasting fire, which was prepared for the devil and his angels?*[138] For it is evident that He rebukes them, not because they did not believe in Him, but because they did not perform good works. In fact, this is why He said that He will separate all who were united together by the same faith, in order that no one might think that faith alone, or a dead faith, that is, a faith without works, is sufficient for eternal life, and in order to make it clear that they who will say to Him: *Lord, when did we see you* suffering this and that and *did not minister to you?*[139] will be those who had believed in Him but had neglected to do good works—as though it were possible to obtain eternal life by a faith that is dead.

Or, perhaps, they think that those persons will go into eternal fire who have not performed works of mercy, but those will not who have robbed others or who have desecrated the temple of God within them and thus have been unmerciful to themselves.[140] As if works of mercy could be of any merit without charity, for as the Apostle says: *If I should distribute all my goods to the poor and have not charity, it profits me nothing.*[141] Nor can one love his neighbor as himself if he does not love himself, for *he who loves iniquity hates his own soul.*[142] And as regards the fire of hell, let us not deceive ourselves, as some do, in thinking that the fire itself is eternal but not the punishment. These say that those who will be saved by fire, that is, those who had faith but did not perform good works, will certainly undergo the punishment of fire, but this punishment will not be for eternity, because, though the fire itself is eternal, they will not burn in it forever.[143] But the Lord, since He is the Lord and foresees all, foresees this also, and therefore He concludes his statement by saying: *Thus these shall go into everlasting punishment, but the just into life everlasting.*[144] It is evident, therefore, that the punishment will be eternal the same as the fire, and that the Truth has said that they will suffer this punishment who, though they had faith, did not perform good works.

26. If all these passages, therefore, and the many other innumerable passages throughout Scripture that are just as clear, if all these are false, then their interpretation of St. Paul's statement regarding the wood, hay, and stubble could be true, namely, that those will be saved by fire who only believed in Christ but neglected to do good works. However, if these passages are both true and clear, then without any doubt whatever we must look for another interpretation of the Apostle's statement. Moreover, if these passages are true and clear, then we must admit that there are in the writings of St. Paul, as St. Peter says, some things hard to understand, and that this statement is one of them. But because it is hard to understand, we should not on that account interpret it to our own ruin, as, for example, to say, in open contradiction to the teaching of Scripture, that those who live very evil lives can be sure of obtaining salvation, even if they stubbornly persist in their evil ways and do not change for the better or repent for their sins.

Chapter 16

Augustine's interpretation of 1 Cor. 3.11–15.

27. Here perhaps I might be asked what I think of this passage from St. Paul and how I think it should be interpreted. Let me say that I would rather hear others more intelligent and more learned than myself explain this passage, but explain it in such a way that all those scriptural texts which I quoted above, and whatever others I did not quote, would remain true and unchanged in their meaning. For these texts tell us very clearly that only that faith is of value *which*, as the Apostle says, *works by charity*,[145] or, in other words, that faith cannot save without good works, whether with fire or without fire; for, if it saves by fire, then certainly it is by faith alone that we are saved. But on this matter Scripture is perfectly clear. *What does it profit*, says St. James, *if a man say he has faith, but has not works? Shall faith be able to save him?*[146] However, I will give, as briefly as possible, my own opinion of this difficult passage of St. Paul.[147] But let it be kept well in mind what I have said above, namely, that I would prefer to hear others more competent than myself.

The foundation, which is Christ, is the construction of a wise architect. This does not need any explaining, for it is clearly said: *For other foundation no man can lay but that which is laid, which is Christ Jesus.*[148] But if Christ is the foundation, then there is no doubt whatever that we must have faith in Christ, since it is *by faith*, as the same Apostle says, that Christ dwells *in our hearts.*[149] Furthermore, if we must have faith in Christ, then certainly it must be that faith which, as the Apostle has defined it, *works by love.*[150] But that faith which the devils have—for they too believe and tremble and acknowledge that Jesus is the Son of God[151]—that faith, I say, cannot be considered as belonging to the foundation. Why not? Because it is not faith which acts through love, but faith which is expressed through fear. The faith, therefore, of Christ, the faith of Christian grace, that is, the faith which acts through love, this faith, if laid on the foundation, allows no one to be lost. But what does it mean to build on this foundation gold, silver, precious stones, wood, hay, and stubble? If I should try to explain more exactly what this passage means, I am afraid that my explanation might be all the harder to understand. Nevertheless, I will try, with God's help, to explain briefly and as clearly as I can what I think this passage means.

Consider the man who asked the good Lord what he should do to obtain eternal life. And when the Lord said to him that, if he wished to come to life, he should keep the commandments, he asked Him: What commandments? The Lord said to him: *You shall not kill, you shall not commit adultery, you shall not steal, you shall not bear false witness, honor your father and your mother, and you shall love your neighbor as yourself.*[152] If he kept these and had faith in Christ, then without any doubt whatever he would have that faith which acts through love. Besides, he would not love his neighbor as himself unless he also loved God, for, if he did not love God, he would not love himself. Furthermore, if he did that other thing also which the Lord spoke to him, namely, *If you will be perfect, go, sell all that you have and give to the poor and you shall have treasure in heaven; and come, follow me,*[153] then he would build on the foundation gold, silver, and precious stones, for in that case he would not think anything except *the things that are of God, how he might please God.*[154] And these thoughts are, in my opinion, the gold, the silver, and the precious stones.

However, if he were inordinately attached to his wealth, even though he gave much of it away in alms, and even though he did not try to increase it by fraud or theft, nor committed any sin or crime from fear of losing it or a part of it—to do otherwise would mean to remove himself from the foundation—but, as I said, if he were inordinately attached to his wealth, and because of this attachment found it painful to part with it, then he would build on the foundation wood, hay, and stubble. Especially would this be true if he had a wife whom he was so anxious to please that he would be solicitous *for the things of the world, how he may please his wife.*[155] If these things are loved with an inordinate affection, it is hard to part with them. He, therefore, who is inordinately attached to them, even though he has faith in Christ who is the foundation, and has that faith which *works by charity,*[156] and although he does not in any way whatever esteem or love them more than his faith, nevertheless, if he has to part with them, their loss causes him pain, and this pain is, as it were, the fire by which he is saved. But the less one is attached to them, or, in possessing them, if one possesses them as though he did not possess them, the less pain he suffers in parting with them. However, he who commits murder, adultery, fornication, idolatry, and other similar sins in order to retain or acquire these things, such a person will not be saved by fire because of the foundation, but rather, having separated himself from the foundation, he will burn in everlasting fire.

28. But our opponents would prove to us how powerful faith is of itself from these words of St. Paul: *But if the unbeliever depart, let him depart; for a brother or sister is not under servitude in such cases.*[157] They take these words to mean that, for the sake of the faith of Christ, a man is permitted to leave his lawful wife if she refuses to live with him as a Christian precisely because he is a Christian. But what they overlook is that a man is perfectly justified in leaving his wife, provided she should say to him: I will not be your wife, unless you rob to make me rich, or unless you allow lewd practices to continue in our house. Or he is justified in leaving her if she demands that, even as a Christian, he continue in some disgraceful or evil practice in order that she might satisfy her lust, or that she might have a better living, or finer clothes to wear.[158] If a wife speaks in this way to her husband, and if, nevertheless, when he comes to be baptized, he is truly sorry for his sins and has that faith in Christ which works by love, then there is no doubt whatever that he loves God more than his wife, and that he will not hesitate to cut off any member that is a scandal to him. But if he finds it painful to leave his wife because of carnal attachment to her, then this is the pain he will suffer, this is the fire in which the hay will burn and by which he will be saved. If, on the contrary, he loved his wife with a pure love,[159] if his love for her was not carnal, if he loved her in the hope that he might help to save her soul, and if he rendered the debt of marriage rather than asked for it, then there is no doubt that he will not find it painful to leave her; for in loving her he thought only of *the things that are of God, how he might please God.*[160] Therefore, the more gold, silver, and precious stones that a man builds on the foundation by reason of such thoughts, the less hay there will be in his building and the less his building will burn.

29. Whether men suffer these afflictions in this life only, or in the next life also,[161] this interpretation of St. Paul's words is not, in

my judgment, contrary to truth. But even if there is another interpretation of which I am not aware, and which one would prefer, nevertheless, as long as we hold to this one, we are not forced to say to the unjust, to the disobedient, the wicked, the impure, to parricides, matricides, murderers, fornicators, to homosexuals, menstealers, liars, perjurers, *and whatever other thing is contrary to sound doctrine which is according to the gospel of the glory of the blessed God:*[162] all that is necessary is that you believe in Christ and receive His sacrament of baptism, and you will be saved, even though you continue to lead very wicked lives.

30. But our opponents object. They say that the Lord granted the Canaanite woman her request, though at first He had refused her in these words: *It is not good to take the bread of the children and to cast it to the dogs.*[163] But the Lord, the searcher of hearts, finally granted the woman her request and praised her because He saw that she was converted. Besides, he did not say to her: "O dog, great is your faith," but: *O woman, great is your faith.*[164] He spoke to her in a different manner the second time because He saw that she was converted and that she had profited by His rebuke. I would certainly be surprised if He praised her for a faith that lacked good works, that is, a faith that did not act by love, a dead faith, a faith which the apostle James did not in the least hesitate to say was a faith not of Christians but of devils. But if our opponents are not willing to admit that the Canaanite woman renounced her evil ways when Christ showed His contempt for her and rebuked her, then let them do as Christ did. Christ healed the daughter of the Canaanite woman; let them heal, if they can, the children of those who believe only, of those who refuse to renounce their evil ways, who, far from concealing their evil lives, even go so far as to willingly profess them. But let them take care that they do not allow such persons to become members of Christ as long as they are willing to remain members of a prostitute. They are right, certainly, in saying that anyone who, to the very end of his life, refuses to believe in Christ commits a sin against the Holy Spirit and that his sin will not be forgiven him for all eternity,[165] provided, however, that they understand correctly what it really means to believe in Christ. For the faith that saves is not the faith which the devils have and which is correctly called a dead faith, but the faith *which works by charity.*[166]

CHAPTER 17

Persons who commit serious sins and who are not willing to give up such sins must not be allowed to receive baptism.

31. Therefore, when we do not admit such persons to baptism, it is not because we wish to root out the cockle before the harvest; on the contrary, we do not wish to imitate the devil and sow cockle amongst the wheat. It is not we who keep them from coming to Christ; rather, we prove to them from their own lips that it is they who do not wish to come to Christ. We do not forbid them to believe in Christ, but we show them that it is they who do not want to believe in Christ, since they deny that that is adultery which Christ says is adultery, and since they think that they who commit adultery can become members of Christ, whereas the Apostle says that such persons will not possess the kingdom of God and that they are opposed to *sound doctrine which is according to the gospel of the glory of the blessed God.*[167] Consequently, these persons are not to be numbered among those who came to the wedding banquet, but among those who refused to come.[168] And since they openly contradict the doctrine of Christ and are opposed to the teaching of the holy Gospels, it is not we therefore who hold them back from coming, but it is they themselves who do not care to come.

There are those, on the other hand, who renounce the world at least in word, if not in fact. These come, to be sure, and they are planted with the wheat, they are stored away in the granary, they are joined to the sheep, they are caught in the nets, and they are seated at the banquet table together with the other guests.[169] But with these the case is different. Once they are received into the Church, whether we discover or do not discover that they are insincere, then we must tolerate them if it is impossible to correct them and if there is no good reason for cutting them off. But let no one think that, because the Scriptures say that there were brought to the wedding feast *all that they found, both good and bad*,[170] this means therefore that they brought those who were obstinate in evil. If that were the case, we would have to say that it was the master's own servants who planted the cockle and that, consequently, the Scriptures are false in saying that *the enemy that sowed them is the devil.*[171] But since the Scriptures cannot be false, we must say then that the *servants* brought in *both good and bad* because the bad were either not known or were discovered only after they were brought in. Or *good and bad* might mean here that these people were judged good or bad by their fellow men, for even amongst nonbelievers men are praised or censured for what they are. This is why the Lord advised His disciples, when He sent them for the first time to preach the gospel, that *into whatever city* they came they should find out *who in it is worthy*,[172] so that they might dwell with him until their departure. And, in fact, is not that man worthy who is considered a good man by his fellow citizens? And is not that man unworthy who is known to them as a bad man? Those who come to Christ are of both kinds, and thus the bad are brought in as well as the good, since they are willing to do penance for their evil works. But if they refuse to do penance, then it is not we who do not allow them to enter. Rather, it is they themselves who will not enter, since they declare openly that they will not renounce their evil deeds.

32. Therefore, that servant who will not make use of the Lord's talent will not be punished or condemned as lazy,[173] since in truth it is they who do not want to receive the talent that He would pay out to them. Besides, this parable is meant for those who refuse to take on the office of steward in the Church, giving as an excuse for their laziness that they do not want to be held accountable for the sins of others, of those who hear and do not put into practice, that is, of those who receive and do not make a return. But the faithful and zealous steward, the steward who is always ready to make use of the Lord's talent, who is most eager to acquire gain for the Lord, this steward says to the adulterer: "Do not commit adultery if you wish to be baptized; believe in Christ if you wish to be baptized, in Christ who condemns your action as a sin of adultery; do not give yourself to a prostitute if you wish to become a member of Christ."[174] If he says: "No, I will not do what you ask," then it is not the steward who is to blame, but he himself; for it is evident that he does not want to receive the Lord's talent, but wants instead to deposit his own false money in the treasury

of the Lord. But if he says that he will do what he is asked and does not do it, and cannot afterwards be brought to repent, then a way should be found of disposing of him so that, if he cannot be of benefit to himself, he might not do harm to others. If he is a bad fish in the good nets of the Lord, still he should not be allowed to ensnare the fishes of the Lord in evil nets. I mean that, if he is living an evil life in the Church, care should be taken that he does not introduce any false teaching in the Church. If we admit to baptism persons who defend their evil deeds, and who declare openly that they will continue to commit them, then we might as well say that fornicators and adulterers, even if they commit those sins till the end of their lives, will possess the kingdom of God, and that they will be saved and obtain eternal life by faith alone, that is, a faith without works, a faith that is dead.[175]

These are the evil nets which the fishermen especially must guard against, that is, if by fishermen in the Gospel parable is meant the bishops and other ministers of lower rank who rule over the churches,[176] for it is said: *Come, and I will make you fishers of men.*[177] Both good and bad fish can be caught in the nets of the Church, but only bad fish in the nets of evil. For if a doctrine is morally good, he who accepts it and puts it into practice is good; he who accepts it and does not put it into practice is evil. But if a doctrine is morally bad, both he who accepts it, even though he does not put it into practice, is evil, and he who puts it into practice is worse.

Chapter 18

Continuation of same theme as in chapter 17.

33. We have here an opinion which, whether of recent or of earlier times, is, at any rate, pernicious and ought to be rejected. But the amazing thing is that they who hold this opinion say that it is rather we who are introducing something new in not admitting to baptism men whose morals are of the worst kind and who declare publicly

that they will continue to live in sin. But go where they will, they will not find anywhere that the Church admits to her sacraments prostitutes, actors,[178] or any disreputable person[179] unless he first abandon his evil ways. Yet these men would permit such persons to receive the sacraments if it were not that the Church has always held to the old and strict practice of not admitting them, a practice based on that most clear and certain truth, namely, that *they who do such things shall not possess the kingdom of God.*[180] In a word, the Church does not allow such persons to receive baptism unless they are willing to do penance for their sins. But if the Church unsuspectingly admits any such person to baptism, even so he cannot be saved unless he repents and does penance.

Concerning persons who commit sins of drunkenness, avarice, calumny,[181] or any other detestable sin of this kind, if they cannot be proved guilty of these sins, nevertheless it should be pointed out to them in their instructions that such sins are severely condemned by the laws of Christian morality and that those who commit them are not permitted to receive baptism unless they show a change for the better. But as for persons who live in adultery, that is, who live with the husband or wife of another—an evil which is condemned not by human law but by divine law—if in some places they have been admitted through negligence, then this is an abuse which we ought to correct by taking example from the Church, that is, we should refuse to admit these also along with those mentioned above. Certainly we are not taking example from the Church, rather we are substituting evil for good, when we say that the *competentes* should not be taught the moral obligations demanded of a Christian. It is no wonder, then, that they who hold this opinion think that everyone should be admitted to baptism, including even those whose lives are a public scandal, for example, prostitutes, panders, gladiators,[182] and others of this sort. According to them, these persons should be admitted, even if they refuse to abandon their evil ways. But these sins, and all those, in fact, which the Apostle mentions and concerning which he says that *they who do such things shall not possess the kingdom of God*, all these zealous pastors ought to condemn.[183] They should rebuke, as the case merits, anyone who they know is guilty of any of these sins, and if he will not amend, he should not be admitted to baptism.

Chapter 19

Three sins which are mortally sinful: impurity, idolatry, and homicide.

34. Some are of the opinion that sin is easily atoned for by the giving of alms.[184] But even these have no doubt at all that there are three sins which are mortally sinful, namely, impurity, idolatry, and homicide.[185] And they do not hesitate to say that he who commits any one of them should be excommunicated[186] until he has sufficiently atoned for his sin.[187] But this is not the place to discuss this opinion or to determine its merits.[188] This would only lengthen our work and is not at all necessary to the solution of our problem. It suffices to say that, if there is any sin for which a person should be refused baptism, that sin is adultery. But if it is maintained that the only sins for which a person should be refused are the three mentioned above, even so, adultery—the reason for this whole discussion—is one of them.

35. The morals of bad Christians of former times were indeed of the worst kind. Yet it seems that this particular evil, namely, men and women marrying the wives and husbands of others, was not one of their vices. This fact may perhaps explain why some churches in their instructions to the *competentes* neglected to question[189] them concerning this evil, and why therefore they did not condemn it. As a result, some began to think that there was nothing wrong in such conduct. However, this sin is not as yet common amongst Christians, unless we make it so by our negligence. Such negligence on the part of some, lack of experience on the part of others, and ignorance in still others is perhaps what our Lord meant by sleep when he said: *While men were asleep, the enemy came and oversowed cockle.*[190]

It seems, therefore, that this particular sin was not one of the sins of bad Christians of former times, since St. Cyprian does not mention it in his letter *De lapsis*,[191] though he deplores and reproves here many of the evils of his time, which evils, he says, have aroused the anger of God and brought down upon the Church an unbearable persecution. He says nothing about it, even though he mentions as one of the evils the marrying of Christians with unbelievers, a union which is nothing else, he says, than a prostitution of the members of Christ.[192] But today such marriages are no longer considered sinful. Since nothing is said against them in the New Testament, it is thought that they are permitted or it is doubted that they are sinful.[193] It is true that some things are doubtful. It is doubtful, for example, whether Herod married his brother's wife while his brother was still alive or after his death,[194] and therefore it is not clear what John the Baptist meant in saying to Herod that it was not lawful for him to have his brother's wife.[195] Likewise, in the case of a woman who promises to have relations only with her paramour, and with no one else even if he abandons her, one has reason to doubt whether she should not be admitted to baptism.[196] Furthermore, the man who leaves his wife because of adultery[197] and marries another is not, it seems, as blameworthy as the man who for no reason leaves his wife and marries another. Nor is it clear from Scripture whether a man who has left his wife because of adultery, which he is certainly permitted to do, is himself an adulterer if he marries again. And if he should, I do not think that he would commit a grave sin.[198] However, there are some marriages which are certainly illicit, and whoever enters into them should not be admitted to baptism unless he amends and does penance. As for doubtful marriages, these we should try to prevent. For what advantage is there in marriages of this kind? But if some are already married in this way, then I am not so sure that we should admit such persons to baptism.

Chapter 20

The proper procedure for admission to baptism.

36. If we are not to give the sinner a false security, or even authorization to commit sin, this then, in accordance with true and sound doctrine, is the procedure we must follow in our instructions, namely, that all who are to be baptized are to believe in God the Father, Son, and Holy Spirit, as is prescribed in the Creed;[199] that they are to do penance for their sins; and that they are not to doubt that

all their past sins will be forgiven them when they receive baptism. They must be told that this forgiveness is not a license to commit sin, but a release from sin; that it is a remission of sin, not a permission to sin. Then it can be truly said of them, in a spiritual sense: *Behold, you are made whole; sin no more.*[200] For though the Lord, when He spoke these words, was referring to physical sickness, He knew too that this sickness in the man whom He healed was a punishment for sin. But I do not see how our opponents can say to a man: *Behold, you are made whole*, if they allow him to receive baptism as an adulterer and to remain an adulterer after baptism. For if adultery is not a disease, and a serious and fatal disease, then I do not know what is.

Chapter 21

Augustine answers more objections.

37. But our opponents object. They say that in the three thousand whom the apostles baptized in one day, and that in the many thousands whom the Apostle evangelized from Jerusalem to Illyria,[201] there were certainly some who were living in adultery, both men and women, and that, consequently, the apostles would have drawn up a law for the churches to follow in determining whether such persons should be admitted to baptism if they would not amend their evil ways. In answer to them, we say that they have not mentioned anyone from this number who was of this sort and who was admitted to baptism. Besides, it would be impossible to mention the sins of each and every man; this would be an endless task. The general norm laid down by St. Peter is adequate and more than adequate. He said to those who were seeking to be baptized: *Save yourselves from this wicked world.*[202] What man doubts that adultery and those who choose to live in adultery are a part of the wickedness of this world?

We could say, moreover, that there were many professional prostitutes amongst those thousands of Christians spread throughout the world, and that therefore the apostles should have made a law regarding their admission or rejection. Nevertheless, we know that no church admits them to baptism unless they abandon their disgraceful practice. Furthermore, from matters of lesser importance we can infer matters of greater importance. If the publicans, for example, who came to be baptized by John[203] were forbidden to receive more tax than they should,[204] then I would indeed be surprised if those who came to receive the baptism of Christ were permitted to live in adultery.

38. But our opponents insist. They say that the Israelites committed many serious offenses and murdered many a prophet; nevertheless, it was not on account of these crimes that they were totally destroyed, but solely because they refused to believe in Christ. But our opponents do not consider that this was not the only sin which the Jews committed against Christ; it must also be remembered that they put Christ to death. The one is a sin of unbelief, the other a sin of cruelty. The one, therefore, is contrary to faith, the other to good morals. But he who has the faith of Christ is free from both these vices. I do not mean a faith that is dead, a faith without works which even the devils have,[205] but that faith which is enlivened by grace, that faith which *works by charity.*[206]

39. This is that faith of which it is said: *The kingdom of heaven is within you.*[207] This kingdom they take by force who believe and who do violence to themselves, who ask for and receive the spirit of love, for love is the *fulfilling of the law.*[208] Without love the law is a dead letter; without love the law makes man a transgressor of the law. But we must not think that the saying, *The kingdom of heaven suffers violence and they who do violence bear it away,*[209] means that the wicked who believe only, but do not lead a good life, will obtain the kingdom of heaven. It means rather that man is freed by faith from that transgression of the law which is caused by the law itself, that is, when the law is enforced in the letter only. It means also that they who believe and do violence to themselves receive the Holy Spirit, whose love *is poured forth in our hearts,*[210] and through whom the law is fulfilled not from fear of punishment but from love of justice.

CHAPTER 22

What it means to know God.

40. Let no one, therefore, deceive himself in thinking that he knows God if his faith in God is dead, that is, devoid of good works like that of the devils. And let no one think that he is assured of eternal life because of what the Lord says, namely, *This is eternal life, that they may know you, the only true God, and Jesus Christ, whom you have sent.*[211] For remember that Scripture also says: *In this we know Him, if we keep His commandments. He who says that he knows Him and keeps not His commandments is a liar and the truth is not in him.*[212] And let no one think that the commandments of God pertain only to faith. But no one has dared to make such an assertion, especially since God actually gave man commandments. And in order that they might not be too many to remember, He reduced them to two when He said: *On these two commandments depend the whole law and the prophets.*[213] However, it can be truthfully said that the commandments of God pertain only to faith, provided that the faith which is meant is not a dead faith but that living faith which works through love. And this is what St. John means, for later on he explains his statement with these words: *This is His commandment, that we should believe in the name of His Son Jesus Christ and love one another.*[214]

41. It is to our advantage, then, to believe in God with the true faith, to worship Him and to know Him, so that we might obtain His help to live a good life, and His pardon if we should sin. But it is not to our advantage to continue to live fearlessly in sin. This means, then, that we should abstain from sin and ask for His help, saying to Him: *I said, O Lord, be merciful to me. Heal my soul, for I have sinned against you.*[215] But those who do not believe in God cannot say this prayer to Him; and they say it in vain who are so separated from Him that they have no share in the grace of the mediator.

Consequently, I do not see how our opponents, blinded as they are by a false security, can hope to understand correctly these words in the book of Wisdom: *And if we sin, we are yours.*[216] For ours is a great and good God who is both willing and able to pardon the sins of repentant sinners, but who also does not hesitate in the least to destroy those who persist in evil. After having said *we are yours*, the inspired writer says *knowing your power*,[217] that power surely from which the sinner cannot flee or hide himself. And therefore he goes on to say: *But we will not sin, for we know that we are yours.*[218] For what man who desires to live in heaven with God, the home of the elect, that is, of those who have been called according to the plan of God,[219] will not try to live a life worthy of heaven? Likewise, when St. John says: *These things I have written to you that you may not sin. And if any man sin, we have an advocate with the Father, Jesus Christ the just; and He is an effectual intercessor for our sins*,[220] he does not mean that we should sin without fear, but that we should repent of our sins if we have committed any, and that we should not at all abandon hope, since we have an advocate whom unbelievers do not have.

Chapter 23

A false interpretation of St. Paul's words in Romans 2.12.

42. We see, then, from these words of St. John that he does not promise any easier condition to those who want to believe in God and at the same time lead a life of sin. Much less does St. Paul when he says: *For whosoever have sinned without the law shall perish without the law; and whosoever have sinned in the law shall be judged by the law.*[221] There is no difference here, as some might think, between "perish" and "judged," since both words mean the same thing. Scripture often uses the word "judgment" for eternal damnation, as, for example, in the Gospel, where the Lord says: *The hour comes wherein all that are in the graves shall hear His voice. And they that have done good things shall come forth unto the resurrection of life; but they that have done evil, unto the resurrection of judgment.*[222] Notice that he does not say here "they who have believed" and "they who have not believed," but *they that have done good things* and *they that have done evil*. For a good life is inseparable

from faith, from that faith *that works by charity;*[223] in fact, they are one and the same. We see, then, that by the resurrection of the judgment the Lord meant the resurrection of eternal damnation. For in speaking of those who will rise again—and this certainly includes unbelievers, since they too will be in their graves[224]—the Lord made two divisions: those who will rise to life and those who will rise to judgment.

43. But our opponents might say that St. Paul does not speak here of unbelievers, but of those who have believed and who therefore will be saved by fire, even though their lives were wicked. They might say that the word "judgment" means here a transitory punishment, which they will undergo who have led wicked lives but who have believed. But this would be a very bold assertion. For the Lord, in speaking of those who will rise, and here he certainly includes unbelievers, divides them into two classes: those who will rise to "life" and those who will rise to "judgment." By judgment He means eternal judgment, although He does not say this in so many words, just as by life He means eternal life, although in this case too He does not mention the word "eternal." He does not say, for example, they will rise to eternal life, but this certainly is what He means.

Furthermore, how do they explain this statement which the Lord makes: *But he who does not believe is already judged.*[225] For without any doubt they must understand judgment here either as eternal punishment, or they will have to say that even unbelievers will be saved by fire, since *he who does not believe*, says the Lord, *is already judged*, that is, is already destined for judgment. If this is the case, then the reward promised those who believe but who live evil lives is not any greater than that of those who do not believe, since they who do not believe will not perish but will be judged. But if they do not dare to make such an assertion, then let them not dare to promise any milder terms to those of whom it is said: *They shall be judged by the law*,[226] for it is evident that the word "judgment" is often used in place of eternal damnation.

And what will they answer if we tell them that those who sin knowingly, far from suffering lesser punishment, will suffer even greater punishment? This is true especially of those who have received the law, for, as it is written, *Where there is no law, neither is there transgression.*[227] And again: *I had not known concupiscence, if the law did not say: You shalt not covet. But sin, taking occasion by the commandment, wrought in me all manner of concupiscence,*[228] and many other passages which the same apostle has on this subject. The grace of the Holy Spirit, obtained for us through Jesus Christ our Lord, frees us from this greater punishment of sin, and, *charity being poured forth in our hearts,*[229] makes us delight in justice and helps us to conquer the excesses of concupiscence. We see, therefore, that the punishment of those *who have sinned in the law [and] shall be judged by the law*[230] is not less severe but more severe than that of those who, having sinned without the law, shall perish without the law.[231] We see, too, that the word "judgment" as used here does not mean a passing punishment but the same kind of punishment which unbelievers will undergo.

44. They who use this sentence to promise salvation by fire to those who believe, but who live evil lives, or, in other words, who say to such persons: *Whosoever have sinned without the law shall perish without the law; and whosoever have sinned in the law shall be judged by the law,*[232] meaning by this that such persons "will not perish but will be saved by fire," I say, they who interpret these words in this way could not have observed that St. Paul was speaking here of those who have sinned without the law, and of those who have sinned in the law. They could not have observed that he was speaking here of the Jews and of the Gentiles, and that he was explaining that the grace of Christ was necessary not only to the Gentiles but to the Jews also, if they desired to be free. This, in fact, is the theme of the Epistle to the Romans. Now, then, let them promise, if they will, salvation by fire to the Jews also, to the Jews who sin in the law and of whom it is said: *They shall be judged by the law.* Let them promise them salvation, even though they are not freed by the grace of Christ, since it is of them that it is said: *They shall be judged by the law.* But if they will not do this, for fear of contradicting themselves, since they accuse the Jews of the serious sin of unbelief, why then, with regard to a subject which pertains to faith in Christ, do they apply to believers and unbelievers what was said of those who have sinned without the law and of those who have sinned in the law? For St. Paul was speaking here of the Jews and of the Gentiles, both of whom he was trying to convert to the grace of Christ.

CHAPTER 24

Continuation of the same.

Furthermore, St. Paul did not say "They who have sinned without faith shall perish without faith; they who have sinned with faith shall be judged by faith." On the contrary, he said: they who have sinned *without the law* and they who sinned *in the law*. It is clearly evident that the problem treated here is one which concerns the Jews and the Gentiles, not one which concerns good and bad Christians.[233]

45. But our opponents would want us to understand that St. Paul is speaking here of faith and not of law—an interpretation which is unthinkable and absurd. But if this is the way they would understand his words, then they would do well to read a certain very clear passage of the apostle Peter. In this passage St. Peter speaks of those who took as a pretext for sins of the flesh and for doing evil those words of Scripture which say that we who belong to the New Testament *are not the children of the bondwoman but of the free, by the freedom wherewith Christ has made us free.*[234] These men thought that, since the redemption gave them security, liberty meant they could do whatever they pleased. But they failed to consider these other words of Scripture, namely: *For you, brethren, have been called unto liberty; only make not liberty an occasion to the flesh.*[235] And therefore St. Peter says: *as free and not as making liberty a cloak for malice.*[236] And in his second epistle he says of them: *These are fountains without water and clouds tossed with whirlwinds, to whom the mist of darkness is reserved. For, speaking proud words of vanity, they allure by the desires of fleshly riotousness those who for a little while escape, such as converse in error, promising them liberty, whereas they themselves are the slaves of corruption. For by whom a man is overcome, of the same also he is the slave. For if, flying from the pollutions of the world through the knowledge of our Lord and Savior Jesus Christ, they be again entangled in them and overcome, their latter state is become unto them worse than the former. For it had been better for them not to have known the way of justice than, after they have known it, to turn back from that holy*

commandment which was delivered to them. For that of the true proverb has happened to them: the dog is returned to his vomit; and the sow that was washed, to her wallowing in the mire.[237] Why, then, in opposition to so evident a truth, do our opponents still promise those who know the way of justice, that is, the Lord Christ, but who live wickedly, a milder punishment than they would receive if they never knew the way of justice? For Scripture says very clearly that *it had been better for them not to have known the way of justice than, after they have known it, to turn back from the holy commandment which was delivered to them.*[238]

Chapter 25

Knowledge of sin brings a greater guilt of sin.

46. The holy commandment mentioned here is not the one which obliges us to believe in God—although everything we must do and believe is contained in this commandment, if we understand by faith that faith *that works by charity.*[239] But the Apostle clearly explains what he means by the holy commandment, namely, that we must renounce the immorality of this world and live righteously. This is what he says: *For if, flying from the pollutions of the world through the knowledge of our Lord and Savior Jesus Christ, they be again entangled in them and overcome, their latter state is become unto them worse than the former.*[240] He does not say "flying from ignorance of God" or "flying from the unbelief of the world" or any such thing, but *flying from the pollutions of the world*, where certainly every kind of immorality exists. And in an earlier passage, in speaking of these men, he said: *feasting together with you, having eyes full of adultery and of sin that ceases not.*[241] He also calls them wells without water: wells, because they have received knowledge of the Lord Christ; without water, because they do not live according to their knowledge. And the apostle Jude has this to say of such men: *These are they who in your feasts of charity, being polluted, feast with you, feeding themselves without fear, clouds without water* and so forth.[242] What

St. Peter says, namely, *feasting together with you, having eyes full of adultery*, this St. Jude says in these words: *These are they who in your feasts of charity, being polluted, feast with you.* In other words, they are mixed with the good in the participation of the sacraments and in the love feasts of the people. St. Peter calls them *fountains without water;* St. Jude, *clouds without water;* and St. James says that their faith is *dead.*[243]

47. Therefore, let us not promise those who live wicked and shameful lives that they will suffer only a temporary punishment of fire because they have known the way of justice. It had been better for them, as Scripture so clearly says, if they had not known it. And the Lord has this to say about such men: *And the last state of that man is made worse than the first.*[244] It is worse because, by not allowing the Holy Spirit to dwell in his soul and to purify it, he invited the unclean spirit to return with more of his kind. Perhaps the men with whom we are concerned here are not as bad as those described above in Scripture. For these men did not turn again to committing adultery—they never gave it up; they did not defile themselves again, once they were made clean—they refused to be made clean. They do not unburden their consciences and renounce their former sins before receiving baptism and then afterwards return to them, like the dog to his vomit. Instead, they obstinately persist in receiving the sacred sacrament with unrepented sin in their hearts. They do not try to conceal their infamy, not even by false promises, but they boldly display it. They do not look back, as did the wife of Lot[245] in leaving Sodom; they absolutely refuse to leave Sodom; still more, they try to bring Christ into Sodom with themselves. Paul the apostle says: *I who before was a blasphemer and a persecutor and unjust; but I obtained mercy because I did it ignorantly in unbelief.*[246] But to these men, whom we have been describing, our opponents say: "Then will you rather obtain mercy, if you sin knowingly, provided you have the faith." But it would be too long and practically impossible to quote all the passages of Scripture which prove that the punishment of those who commit grievous sins knowingly, far from being lighter than that of those who sin in ignorance, is for that very reason more severe. Those we have given are sufficient proof.

CHAPTER 26

Distinction of sins and remedies.

48. Let us take care, therefore, with the help of the Lord God, not to make men falsely secure by saying to them that, as long as they are baptized in Christ and have the faith, they will be saved, no matter what kind of life they lead. Let us not make Christians the way the Jews make proselytes, concerning whom the Lord says: *Woe to you, scribes and Pharisees, who compass sea and land to make one proselyte, but after you have made him, you make him the child of hell twofold more than yourselves.*[247] Let us rather hold fast to the true doctrine of God, our Master, holding fast to both these truths, namely, that a Christian's life should harmonize with the sacred character of the sacrament of baptism, and that eternal life should not be promised to anyone who is either not baptized[248] or not leading a good life. For it is Christ who said: *Unless a man be born again of the Holy Spirit, he will not enter into the kingdom of heaven.*[249] And it is Christ who also said: *Unless your justice abound more than that of the scribes and Pharisees, you shall not enter into the kingdom of heaven.*[250] And concerning these same scribes and Pharisees He says: *The scribes and Pharisees sit on the chair of Moses; what things they say, do; but what they do, do not.*[251] Their righteousness, therefore, consists in "saying and not doing." It is evident from this reproach that our Lord wills that our righteousness abound more than the "saying and doing" of the scribes and Pharisees; if it does not, we will not enter the kingdom of heaven.

This does not mean that we should so flatter ourselves—to say nothing of boasting to others—as to think that we are free from sin in this life. For if Christians did not commit sins, and sins so serious that they deserve to be punished with excommunication,[252] St. Paul would not say: *You being gathered together and my spirit: to deliver such a one to Satan for the destruction of the flesh, that the spirit may be saved in the day of the Lord Jesus.*[253] And in another place he says: *lest I mourn many that sinned before and have not done penance for the uncleanness and fornication that they have committed.*[254] Likewise, if they did not commit offenses which, although they are not so serious as to be punished by that penance which the Church imposes on her penitents,[255] are nevertheless deserving of correction,[256] the Lord Himself would not say: *Rebuke him between you and him alone; if he shall hear you, you have gained your brother.*[257] Finally, if human life were free of all imperfections, the Lord would not have taught us to ask daily for forgiveness in the Lord's Prayer, in which we say: *Forgive us our debts, as we forgive our debtors.*[258]

Chapter 27

Recapitulation.

49. We have, we believe, sufficiently set forth our views concerning this whole discussion which comprised three questions. The first question had to do with the mingling of good and bad in the Church, which is prefigured in the Gospel by the parable of the cockle and the wheat. In treating this question, we pointed out that we must not interpret these similes, as, for example, the one just mentioned, or that of the unclean animals in the ark, or any other pertaining to this same problem, as meaning that the discipline of the Church should be relaxed. For the Church is like that woman in Proverbs of whom it is said: *The ways of her house are severe.*[259] On the other hand, strict discipline does not mean that we should be so foolish and so rash as to start troublesome schisms in the Church by presuming, for example, that we can separate the good from the bad. We also pointed out that these similes and predictions are not to be taken as an excuse for laziness. They are not to be interpreted as meaning that the good in the Church should neglect to correct whatever evils are in the Church, but rather that they should preserve intact the true doctrine of the Church, and that they should bear patiently whatever evils they cannot correct. Likewise, when Scripture says that unclean animals entered Noah's ark, we are not to understand by this that those in authority should allow sinners to be baptized if they have no respect for so sacred a sacrament, or, what

is far worse, if they intend to continue living in adultery. The entering of unclean animals into the ark was a prediction that there would be evil men in the Church and that they should be tolerated, but without allowing any corruption of doctrine or breakdown of discipline. For the unclean animals did not force their way into the ark, nor did they enter by whatever entrance they pleased, but through the one entrance which Noah had built.

The second question had to do with the instructions given to catechumens. Our opponents say that those who are preparing to receive baptism should be taught only what they must believe. After they are baptized they can be taught what they must do to live a good, Christian life. But we proved sufficiently, if we are not mistaken, that the proper time to speak to them of the punishment which the Lord threatens to inflict on those who live evil lives is when they come for instructions, for then they are eager and anxious to hear what the Church has to say. Then is the time to tell them that they should not receive baptism with serious sin on their souls, a sacrament which they come to receive that their sins might be taken away.

In the third question we discussed an opinion that is very dangerous, an opinion which would not have developed, it seems to us, if more thought had been given it and if it had been studied in connection with Scripture.[260] This is that opinion which says that they who live most evil and most disgraceful lives, even though they continue to live in this way, will be saved and will gain eternal life as long as they believe in Christ and receive His sacraments. This is a flat contradiction of what the Lord said to the man who asked what he must do to gain eternal life: *If you will enter into life, keep the commandments.*[261] The Lord then went on to enumerate the commandments which he must keep.[262] But our opponents, strange to say, promise eternal life to those who commit the very sins which these commandments forbid, provided they have faith, even though it is a dead faith, a faith without works.

These, then, are the three questions which we have discussed and, as we believe, sufficiently discussed. In our treatment of them we pointed out that, although we should tolerate evil men who are in the Church, we should not neglect to enforce discipline in the Church; that those who are preparing for baptism should be instructed not only in what they must believe but also in what they must do; that we should not tell the faithful that they will obtain eternal life if their faith is dead,[263] if it is without works and therefore cannot save, but rather that they will obtain eternal life if they have that faith of grace *that works by charity.*[264] We should not, therefore, accuse those in authority of indifference or negligence if they are faithful in the performance of these duties. Rather, we should reproach those who are so obstinate that they refuse to accept the Lord's money, and who even force His ministers to use their own false money. These men are worse sinners than those mentioned by St. Cyprian.[265] They renounced the world at least in word, if not in fact. But these do not renounce the works of the devil even in word, for they declare openly that they will continue to live in adultery. If there is any saying of our opponents which we may have omitted in this discussion, it is either because we did not think that it pertained to the discussion, or thought that it was so easy to refute that anyone could refute it.

NOTES

LIST OF ABBREVIATIONS

ACW	Ancient Christian Writers
CSEL	Corpus scriptorum ecclesiasticorum latinorum
MG	Patrologia graeca, ed. J. P. Migne
ML	Patrologia latina, ed. J. P. Migne

Bibliography

Adam, K., *Die geheime Kirchenbusse nach dem hl. Augustin: Eine Auseinandersetzung mit B. Poschmann* (Kempten 1921).

Arand, L. A., *St. Augustine: Faith, Hope, and Charity* (ACW 3; Westminster, Md. 1947).

Badcock, F. J., "Le Credo primitif d'Afrique," *Rev. bén.* 45 (1933) 3–9.

Bardy, G., "Manichéisme," *Dict. de théol. cath.* 9.2 (Paris 1926) 1841–95.

Bareille, G., "Catéchuménat," *Dict. de théol. cath.* 2.2 (3rd ed. Paris 1923) 1968–1987.

Bareille, G., "Baptême d'après les Pères grecs et latins," ibid. 2.1, 178–219.

Barreau, M. H., *Oeuvres complètes de saint Augustin* 21 (Paris 1869) 242–86.

Battifol, P., *Le catholicisme de saint Augustin* (4th ed. Paris 1929).

Bergauer, P., *Der Jakobusbrief bei Augustinus und die damit verbündenen Probleme der Rechtfertigungslehre* (Vienna 1962).

Bernard, R., "La prédestination du Christ total selon saint Augustin," *Recherches augustiniennes* 3 (Études augustiniennes; Paris 1965) 1–58.

Boissier, G., *La fin du paganisme* (Paris 1891).

Bourke, V. J., *Augustine's Quest of Wisdom* (Milwaukee 1945).

Burkitt, F. C., *The Religion of the Manichees* (Cambridge 1925).

Burleigh, J. H. S., "St. Augustine on Baptism," *Reformed Theological Review* 15 (1956) 65–80.

Busch, B., *De initiatione christiana secundum doctrinam sancti Augustini* (Rome 1939).

Chéné, J., *La théologie de saint Augustin: Grace et prédestination* (Lyons 1961).

Christopher, J. P., *St. Augustine: The First Catechetical Instruction* (ACW 2; Westminster, Md. 1946).

Combes, G., *La charité d'après saint Augustin* (Paris 1934).
Combes, G., *Oeuvres de saint Augustin* 2: *Problèmes moraux* (Paris 1937).
Cornish, C. L., *Seventeen Short Treatises of S. Augustine* (A Library of Fathers of the Holy Catholic Church 6; Oxford 1847) 37–84.
de Groot, I. F., *Conspectus historiae dogmatum* 1 (Rome 1931).
de Labriolle, P., *History and Literature of Christianity from Tertullian to Boethius* (New York 1925).
de Puniet, P., "Baptême," *Dict. d'archéol. chrét. et de liturg.* 2.1 (Paris 1910).
Dölger, F. J., "Der Durchzug durch das Rote Meer als Sinnbild der christlichen Taufe," *Antike und Christentum* 2 (1930) 63–69.
Duchesne, L., *Christian Worship: Its Origin and Evolution* (London 1903).
Durkin, E. F., *The Theological Distinction of Sins in the Writings of St. Augustine* (Mundelein, Ill. 1952).
Eger, H. *Die Eschatologie Augustins* (Greifswald 1933).
Eichenseer, C. P., *Das Symbolum apostolicum beim heiligen Augustinus, mit Berücksichtigung des dogmengeschichtlichen Zusammenhangs* (St. Ottilien 1960).
Fliche-Martin, *Histoire de l'église* (Paris 1947).
Galtier, P., *L'Église et la rémission des péchés aux premiers siècles* (Paris 1932).
Galtier, P., *De poenitentia: Tractatus dogmatico-historicus* (Paris 1931).
Gatterer, M., *Katechetik* (2nd ed. Innsbruck 1911).
Gendreau, A. J., *Sancti Augustini doctrina de baptismo* (Baltimore 1939).
Geoghegan, A. T., *The Attitude toward Labor in Early Christianity and Ancient Culture* (Washington, D.C. 1945).
Gilson, E., *Introduction á l'étude de saint Augustin* (2nd ed. Paris 1943).
Grabowski, S. J., *The Church: An Introduction to the Theology of Saint Augustine* (St. Louis 1957).
Grabowski, S. J., "The Role of Charity in the Mystical Body of Christ according to Saint Augustine," *Revue des études augustiniennes* 3 (1957) 29–63.
Grabowski, S. J., "Sinners and the Mystical Body of Christ according to St. Augustine," *Theol. Studies* 8 (1947) 614–67; 9 (1948) 47–84.

Grabowski, S. J., "St. Augustine and the Doctrine of the Mystical Body of Christ," *Theol. Studies* 7 (1946) 72–125.

Hamman, A., "Le Nôtre Père dans la catéchèse des Pères de l'église," *Maison Dieu* 85 (1966) 41–68.

Hefele-Leclercq, *Histoire des conciles* 1.1 (Paris 1907).

Hugo, J. J., *St. Augustine on Nature, Sex, and Marriage* (Chicago 1969).

Jacquin, A. M., "La prédestination d'après saint Augustin," *Miscellanea agostiniana* 2 (Rome 1931) 853–78.

Jay, P., "Saint Augustin et la doctrine du purgatoire," *Recherches de théologie ancienne et médiévale* 36 (1969) 17–30.

Jepson, J. J., *St. Augustine: The Lord's Sermon on the Mount* (ACW 5; Westminster, Md. 1948).

Kelly, J. N. D., *Early Christian Doctrines* (3rd ed. London 1965).

Kelly, J. N. D., *Early Christian Creeds* (3rd ed. London 1972).

Krebs, E., "Rechtfertigung," *Lexikon für Theologie und Kirche* (Freiburg im Breisgau 1936) 675–80.

Kuiters, R., "Saint Augustin et l'indissolubilité du mariage," *Augustiniana* 9 (1959) 5–11.

La Bonnardière, A. M., "Pénitence et réconciliation des pénitents d'après saint Augustin," *Rev. des étud. august.* 1–2 (1967) 31–53, 249–283.

La Bonnardière, A. M., "Les commentaires simultanés de Mat. 6,12 et de 1 Jo. 1,8 dans l'oeuvre de saint Augustin," ibid. 1 (1955) 129–147.

Ladomérszky, N., *Saint Augustin, docteur du mariage chrétien* (Rome 1942).

Lagrange, M. J., *Évangile selon saint Matthieu* (2nd ed. Paris 1923).

Landgraf, A., "1 Cor. 3.10–17 bei den lateinischen Vätern und in der Frühscholastik," *Biblica* 5 (1924) 140–72.

Lehaut, A., *L'Éternité des peines de l'enfer dans s. Augustin* (Paris 1912).

Liguori, Sr. M., *Saint Augustine: Treatises on Marriage and Other Subjects* (Fathers of the Church 27; New York 1955) 213–82.

Mangenot, E., "Blasphème contre le Saint Esprit," *Dict. de théol. cath.* 2.1 (3rd ed. Paris 1923) 910–16.

Mansi, J., *Sacrorum conciliorum nova et amplissima collectio* (Florence 1759–98).

Martin, J., *Saint Augustin* (2nd ed. Paris 1923).

Mausbach, J., *Die Ethik des heiligen Augustinus* (Freiburg i. Br. 1929).

Mitterer, S., *Des heiligen Kirchenvaters Aurelius Augustinus ausgewählte praktische Schriften, homiletischen und katechetischen Inhalts* (Bibliothek der Kirchenväter 49; Munich 1925) 312–85.

Moffatt, J., "Augustine on the Lord's Prayer," *Expositor* 18 (1919) 259–72.

Mohrmann, C., *Die altchristliche Sondersprache in den Sermones des hl. Augustin* (Lat. christ. prim. 3; Nijmegen 1932).

Monceaux, P., *Histoire littéraire de l'Afrique chrétienne* 7: *Saint Augustin et le donatisme* (Paris 1923).

Mortimer, R. C., *The Origins of Private Penance in the Western Church* (Oxford 1939).

Musing, H. W., *Augustinus: Lehre von der Taufe* (Diss. Hamburg 1969).

Palmer, P. F., "Jean Morin and the Problem of Private Penance," *Theol. Studies* 6 (1945) 317–57; 7 (1946) 281–308.

Pegon, J., *Oeuvres de saint Augustin* (Bibliothèque augustinienne 8; Paris 1951) 345–461.

Pereira, B. A., *La doctrine du mariage selon saint Augustin* (Paris 1930).

Perl, C. J., *Aurelius Augustinus, Drei Bücher über den Glauben* (Paderborn 1968).

Plumpe, J. C., "Omnia munda mundis," *Theol. Studies* 6 (1945) 509–23.

Pope, H., *St. Augustine of Hippo* (Westminister, Md. 1946).

Portalié, E., "Augustin (Saint)," *Dict. de théol. cath.* 1.2 (3rd ed. Paris 1923) 2268–2472.

Poschmann, B., *Kirchenbusse und Correptio secreta bei Augustinus* (Braunsberg 1923).

Poschmann, B., *S. Aurelii Augustini textus selecti de poenitentia* (Bonn 1934).

Prat, F., *The Theology of Saint Paul* 1–2 (London 1926, 1934).

Quasten, J., *Monumenta eucharistica et liturgica vetustissma* (Bonn 1935, 1937).

Rentschka, P., *Die Dekalogkatechese des hl. Augustinus* (Diss. Breslau 1904).

Reuter, A. O., *Sancti Aurelii Augustini doctrina de bonis matrimonii* (Rome 1942).

Rist, J. M., "Augustine on Free Will and Predestination," in *Augus-*

tine: A Collection of Critical Essays, ed. R. A. Markus (New York 1972) 218–52.
Roland-Gosselin, B., *La morale de saint Augustin* (Paris 1925).
Schanz, M., "Die Lehre des h. Augustinus über die Rechtfertigung," *Theologische Quartalschrift* 83 (1901) 481–528.
Schanz, M., *Geschichte der römischen Litteratur* 4.2 (Munich 1920).
Serrier, G., *De quelques recherches concernant le mariage contrat-sacrement et plus particulierement de la doctrine augustinienne des biens du mariage* 2 (Paris 1928).
Tixeront, J., *History of Dogmas* 1–2 (St. Louis 1910–14).
Tobac, E., "Le problème de la justification dans saint Paul et dans saint Jacques," *Rev. d'hist. eccl.* 22 (1926) 797–805.
Wang, J., *Saint Augustin et les vertus des païens* (Paris 1938).
Weismann, W., *Kirche und Schauspiele* (Würzburg 1972).
Willis, G. G., *St. Augustine and the Donatist Controversy* (London 1950).

Notes to the Introduction

1. Cf. *De fide et operibus* 14.21 ML 40.211: "modo . . . prolixum librum edidi, qui inscribitur, De littera et spiritu." Six manuscripts do not give the word "modo." It is omitted also in the edition of the CSEL (41.62).

2. Cf. *Retract.* 2.37 f. CSEL 36.175 ff.: "In the meantime I received from certain laymen, who, however, were learned in the Scriptures, certain writings which so distinguished good works from Christian faith as to say that it was possible to obtain eternal life without the former but not without the latter. In answer to them I wrote a book which is entitled *On Faith and Works.*" For 413 as the date of composition of the *De fide et operibus*, see the following authors: Portalié, "Augustin (Saint)," DTC 1.2 (1909) 2303; Schanz, *Geschichte* 4.2.420 ff.; Mitterer, *Des heiligen Kirchenvaters Aurelius Augustinus ausgewählte praktische Schriften* 312; Pope, *St. Augustine of Hippo* 376; Perl, *Drei Bücher über den Glauben* xxi. It is worth noting that Perl (XXI) remarks that the writing of the *De fide et operibus* must have been considered important and urgent by Augustine since, at about this time, 413, he was busy with so many other writings, e.g. *De unico baptismo contra Petilianum* in 410, *De spiritu et littera* in 412, and in 413 the beginning of *De civitate Dei*. Besides *Retract.* 2.38, Augustine mentions *De fide et operibus* in three other writings: *Enchir.* 18.67; *De octo Dulcitii quaest.* 1.2; *Ep.* 205.4, 18.

3. Some have thought that these writings were those of St. Jerome, namely, his commentary on Isaias, 66.24 ML 24.677, the *Dialogue against the Pelagians* 1.28 ML 23.544 f., and *Ep.* 119.7 CSEL 55.454 ff. Augustine, however, does not mention any names, and there is no evidence either here or in any other place that he is referring to these passages from the works of Jerome. Nevertheless, both Jerome and Ambrose seemed to have shared in the not uncommon error of their time, namely, that all Christians would sooner or later be reunited to God, an error which Augustine refutes here and in a number of other

places. See Tixeront, *History of Dogmas* 2.339 ff., 346 ff; J. Pegon, *Oeuvres de saint Augustin* 346 ff. See Notes to the Text, n. 4.

4. Cf. *Retract.* 2.38 CSEL 36.177.

5. According to Augustine, it seems that there were two causes which gave rise to this error. The first was a false sympathy for those men and women who were not permitted to receive baptism because they were living in adultery. Rather than see them die without the sacrament and thus suffer eternal punishment, those who sympathized with such persons argued in their behalf and in behalf of all evildoers that these persons could be saved in spite of their evil works, provided they were baptized and had the faith. The second was a false interpretation of the words of St. Paul in 1 Cor. 3.11–15. These words were interpreted to mean that as long as a man had faith in Christ, who is the foundation, he would be saved, even though he built upon this foundation wood, hay, and straw, i.e. works which were evil. The fire would burn his evil works, but this fire was a purifying and saving fire, not a fire that was eternal (*De fide et op.* 1.2; 15.24).

6. See Notes to the Text, n. 37.

7. Cf. Matt. 7.6.

8. See Notes to the Text, n. 2.

9. See Notes to the Text, n. 43.

10. There were a number of errors in the early Church in regard to justification. The antinomians in the time of the apostles advocated a doctrine of justification by faith alone. According to Augustine (*De fide et op.* 14.22), the apostles Peter, John, James, and Jude opposed them in their epistles. Jovinian exaggerated the justifying efficacy of baptism, so much so that he asserted that it was impossible for a baptized person to commit sin (cf. Notes to the Text, n. 34). Pelagianism denied the fact of original sin and saw in sin only a transitory act, not a lasting guilt and a turning away from God. The Pelagian believed that the will could resist evil without any assistance, as, e.g., in the pagan. In the Christian the will was aided in doing good by the example of Christ and by grace, but even in the Christian the will was capable of doing good without the assistance of grace. Thus justification in the Catholic sense had no place whatever in this system. Semi-Pelagianism also taught a false justification. Although it held that justification was obtained through grace which was received in

the sacrament of baptism, nevertheless it taught that the initial preparation for justification was dependent upon the good will of the sinner, previous to any reception of grace. See Krebs, "Rechtfertigung" 678.

11. See Notes to the Text, n. 121.

12. See Notes to the Text, n. 112.

13. See Notes to the Text, n. 115.

14. Cf. Gal. 5.6.

15. 1 Cor. 13.2.

16. Cf. James 2.19.

17. Cf. *De div. quaest.* 76 ML 40.87 ff.; *Enar. in ps.* 31.2 ff. ML 36.259 ff.

18. Cf. *De spiritu et littera* 32.56 ML 44.237.

19. Cf. *De gestis Pel.* 14.34 CSEL 42.89 ff.

20. Cf. *De praed. sanct.* 7.12 ML 44.969.

21. Cf. *De spiritu et littera* 9.15 ML 44.209; *Ep.* 186.3, 7, 10 CSEL 57.50, 53.

22. Cf. *Ep.* 186. 3.7 CSEL 57.50; *De spiritu et littera* 29.51 ML 44.232 ff.

23. Cf. Schanz, "Die Lehre" 485 ff., 492, 509 ff.

Notes to the Text

1. The Greek and Latin Fathers use many expressions to designate the sacrament of baptism. Clement of Alexandria has explained some of them. Baptism, he says, is a bath because it washes away sin; a grace which remits the punishment due to sin; an illumination, since it enables one to contemplate the holy and salutary light; a perfection, because it lacks nothing. Cf. *Paedag.* 1.6 MG 8.282. Augustine calls baptism not only the bath of regeneration but also the sacrament of Christ (*De fide et op.* 12.18), the sacrament of the new life and of eternal salvation (*Cont. Cresc.* 2.13.16 ML 43.476), and the sacrament of the Trinity (*Serm.* 269.2 ML 38.1235). See Bareille, "Baptême" 179 ff.

2. From earliest times the Church has taken care not to confer baptism indiscriminately on everyone who asked for it. She assured herself, first of all, that the candidate was not acting out of mere curiosity or caprice. She demanded of him not only a sincere intention but also knowledge of the principal obligations which this sacrament imposed, obligations with regard to both belief and morals. Moreover, the candidate was obliged to repent of his past sins and to show signs of amendment. Thus, the Church refused to admit to baptism anyone engaged in a profession which was not compatible with the sanctity required of a Christian, e.g. prostitutes, panders, actors, gladiators, idolators, diviners, charioteers, etc. These persons were not admitted unless they first renounced their former way of life. See Bareille, "Baptême" 2.1.191 ff.; Burleigh, "St. Augustine on Baptism" 69 ff.; Musing, *Augustinus Lehre: von der Taufe* 201–4.

3. 1 Cor. 6.15.

4. At the beginning of the fifth century there existed in the Western Church a number of errors which presented salvation as more or less independent of good works, and which denied the eternity of the pains of hell either for all the reprobate or at least for certain classes of sinners. We learn from Augustine the many views—

all of them excessive—which were current among the faithful at this time. Some thought that the pains of hell were to be only temporary for all persons without exception; others, that all would be saved through the intercession of the saints; others, that all who had been baptized and had received the body of the Lord would be saved, even though they were heretics; others promised salvation to all those who had received these two sacraments in the Catholic Church, even though afterwards they had fallen into apostasy and heresy, so that their wickedness, *quanta major fuerit, non eis valeat ad aeternitatem, sed ad diuturnitatem magnitudinemque poenarum*; others thought that only those sinners would be damned to eternal punishment who, while leading sinful lives, had neglected to give alms, whereas the other sinners would be freed from hell sooner or later. Cf. *De civ. Dei* 21.17–22 CSEL 40^2. 548 ff.; *Enchir.* 67, 112 ML 40.263a, 284b; *Enar. in ps.* 80.20 ML 37.1043a; *De octo Dulcitii quaest.* 1 ML 40.149 f. Finally, the error which Augustine mentions here, namely, that all these would be saved who had the faith and were baptized, even though they led wicked lives.

These opinions were held by many Christians: *nonnulli, imo quam plurimi.* Cf. *Enchir.* 67, 112 ML 40.263 f. They were held in the name of God's mercy, and of the redeeming efficacy of the true faith in Jesus. The Christian faith was looked upon as the divine energy which would save all who possessed it; through that faith every Christian was founded upon Christ, and in spite of the wood, hay, and straw, i.e. the evil works which he might build upon this foundation, he would be saved: the fire would destroy his works, but he himself would be spared. The Scripture text very often quoted in support of this view was that of St. Paul, 1 Cor. 3.15. Cf. Tixeront, *History of Dogmas* 2.332 ff., 346; Kelly, *Early Christian Doctrines* 484 ff.

5. 1 Cor. 3.11 f.

6. The Synod of Elvira (306 A.D.) decreed in canon 11 that if a woman catechumen had married a divorced Christian, then the time of her probation for admission to baptism should be extended for five more years. In case of serious sickness she might be baptized earlier. See Hefele-Leclercq, *Histoire des conciles* 1.1.227 f.

7. Cf. Matt. 19.9. Augustine wrote three treatises on marriage. The first, in 400–401, *De bono conjugali*, he wrote against the

heresy of Jovinian, who put marriage on a level with virginity and accused the Catholics of condemning marriage. The second, *De nuptiis et concupiscentia* (419–20), is a defense of marriage against Pelagius, who renewed the accusations of Jovinian. In the third, *De conjugiis adulterinis* (419), Augustine tries to solve, in the light of Scripture, the problem of adulterous marriages. Here he says that adulterers should not be admitted to baptism unless they repent of their sin. In danger of death or in great necessity, if they cannot answer for themselves, they should be baptized so that their sin will be taken away. Cf. *De conj. adult.* 1.28 CSEL 41.381. He shows that marriage is indissoluble even in the case of adultery. The man as well as the woman commits adultery in contracting another marriage. If a man divorces his wife because of fornication, or any other reason, and marries another, he is an adulterer. Cf. ibid. 2.9 CSEL 41.391. Augustine bases his teaching in this matter on St. Paul, 1 Cor. 7.39: *A woman is bound by the law as long as her husband lives.* And Augustine adds: *Ergo consequenter et vir alligatus est, quamdiu mulier ejus vivit. Haec obligatio fuit ut aliis conjugi sine adulterina copulatione non possint* (ibid. 2.9 CSEL 41.391). See B. Roland-Gosselin, *La morale de saint Augustin* 156 ff.; Ladomérszky, *Saint Augustin* 100–106. See also Reuter, *Augustini doctrina de bonis matrimonii;* Pereira, *La doctrine du mariage selon saint Augustin.*

8. Num. 25.5.

9. Num. 25.7 f.

10. Here as elsewhere Augustine teaches that the Church has legislative and coercive power. Legislative power he calls *ecclesiae regimen* (*Cont. Jul.* 3.1.1 ML 44.701). It is the hierarchy that rules the Church, *praepositi, per quos ecclesia nunc gubernatur* (*De civ. Dei* 20.9 CSEL 40^2.451), and the people are those who are ruled, *plebs regenda* (*Ep.* 43.5.16 ML 33.167). The right to govern demands of those who are governed the strict duty to obey: *Pertineat ad nos cura, ad vos obedientia* (*Serm.* 146.1.1 ML 38.796). The coercive power is a consequence of the power of the keys. The Church has received with the keys the right to bind and loose. If anyone despises her reprimands and corrections, let him be, says our Lord, as a heathen and a publican (*De bapt.* 7.51.99 ML 43.241). In regard to the exercise of this right, Augustine describes for us the sanctions of his times by these

terms: *corripiendo, degradando, excommunicando, caeterisque coercitionibus licitis atque concessis, quae salva unitatis pace, in ecclesia quotidie fiunt* (*Post. coll.* 4.6 ML 43.656).

Augustine mentions two kinds of excommunication: one which deprives a person of certain advantages but does not cut him off from the Church, *neque enim a populo Dei separamus, quos vel degradando vel excommunicando ad humiliorem poenitendi locum redigimus* (*Post. coll.* 20.28 ML 43.669); the other which completely cuts off incurable members, *insanabilia membra* (*Ep.* 157.3.22 ML 33.685). This latter type of excommunication is the equivalent in the Church of the death penalty of the Old Law; cf. *Quaest. in Hept.* 5.39 CSEL 28^2.399. See Portalié, "Augustin," DTC 1.2. 2415 ff. See also La Bonnardière, "Pénitence et réconciliation" 44 ff., 196 ff.

11. 2 Cor. 11.26.
12. Phil. 1.15.
13. 1 Cor. 5.1.
14. 1 Cor. 5.5.
15. 1 Tim. 1.20.
16. 1 Cor. 5.9–13.
17. Augustine gives this same interpretation in *Cont. ep. Parm.* 3.2.15 ML 43.94: *auferte, inquit, malum ex vobis ipsis, id est, si non potestis auferre malos ex medio vestrum, ipsum malum auferte ex vobis ipsis. Quodsi quisquam velit sic intelligere, quod dictum est: auferte malum ex vobis ipsis, ut per correptionem separationis de congregatione fratrum malus quisque auferendus sit. . . .* There is no doubt that by *malum* St. Paul understands here the incestuous person mentioned in 1 Cor. 5.1 ff. Nevertheless, in the Latin the meaning is ambiguous; the word *malum* could be either accusative masculine or accusative neuter. The Greek is clear: *eksarate ton ponēron eks hymōn autōn.* Augustine himself makes this observation later on in the second book of the *Retractationes* 2.17 CSEL 36.152, where he says that because of the clearness of the Greek the second meaning only is correct, namely, that the evil man should be expelled by the Church from the society of the good.
18. Augustine had the greatest charity and tolerance for sinners, both for those in the Church and for those outside the Church. "Imitate the good," he says, "tolerate the bad, love all men" (*De cat. rud.* 27.55 ML 40.348). His charity and tolerance towards those outside the Church is best seen in his relations with the Donatists, whom

he had tried to bring back to the Church by every peaceful means possible. It was only when these failed and when the Donatists became abusive and rebellious that he resorted to law and force. For a study of Augustine's tolerance, especially in regard to heretics and schismatics, see Martin, *Saint Augustin* 373–88. For Augustine's relations with the Donatists, see Monceaux, *Histoire littéraire* 7; Bourke, *Augustine's Quest of Wisdom* 138–74.

19. 1 Cor. 5.5.

20. 2 Thess. 3.14 f.

21. Matt. 13.29 f.

22. Matt. 18.15–17.

23. Matt. 18.18.

24. Matt. 7.6.

25. 1 Tim. 5.20.

26. The obligation of fraternal correction, *correctio (correptio) fraterna*, is inculcated by Augustine everywhere in his writings. In the *Sermon on the Mount* (1.20.66 ML 34.1263) he states that correction must not be shunned, that in bringing it to bear we are to use progressively advice (*consilium*), authority (*auctoritas*), and force (*potestas*). We must always be careful in the exercise of this obligation to avoid a penchant for vituperation and condemnation of others. Our correction should be a virtuous, unselfish effort to bring the other person to an improvement of his ways (ibid. 2.19.63 ML 34.1298). Augustine, moreover, wrote a work, *De correptione et gratia*, in which he shows that correction is often necessary, even though in every instance a man's improvement depends upon God's grace. He wrote this book in refutation of the opinion that correction is not necessary and that all we can do for another when he transgresses God's commands is to pray for him. Cf. *Retract.* 2.67 CSEL 36.204. See Jepson, *St. Augustine: The Lord's Sermon on the Mount* 201 n. 65.

27. This is the teaching of the Patripassianists and of Sabellius. See de Groot, *Conspectus historiae dogmatum* 1.109 ff.

28. This is the teaching of the Subordinationists, especially of Arius, but also of Macedonianism and Pneumatomachism. See de Groot, ibid. 1.73, 313, 322 ff.

29. According to the Manichean doctrine, the perfect Manichee carried three seals: the *signaculum oris*, which forbade him impure food, such as the flesh of animals and wine; the *signaculum*

manus, by which he was not allowed to handle certain objects in which the elements of Darkness were contained; and the *signaculum sinus*, which prohibited sexual relations and therefore marriage. The Manichees taught that there were two eternal principles, the Good and the Evil, called also Light and Darkness, God and Satan. Both were omnipotent in their own domain. Satan, after some hard battles, succeeded in seizing a part of the kingdom of light. In order that he might not lose it, he enclosed it in a man, Adam, whom he begot, and to whom he gave for partner a woman, Eve, whom he endowed with the most poisonous portion of the powers of evil. Cf. *De natura boni* 8.46 CSEL 25^2.884 ff. It follows, then, that matrimony is a monstrous union of a portion of God and a portion of Satan. The sensuality which drives the woman to the man is a weapon, forged from all eternity by the Spirit of Evil, to encircle and conquer the Spirit of Good. We must not believe, therefore, that God instituted marriage, and where it exists we must abolish it. One cannot imagine any more horrible act than the conjugal act. Cf. *Cont. litt. Pelagii* 3.9.25 ML 44.607; *De mor. eccl. cath.* 1.35.78–80 ML 32.1343 ff.

Respect for divine holiness thus obliges all believers to preserve virginity. But since this obligation is very difficult because of the repeated assaults of concupiscence, only the elect or the perfect are bound to its strict observance. The simple auditors, who constitute the mass of believers, are permitted, during the period of their purification, to have relations with women and even to marry. But they should not have children, because procreation is the work of the Evil Spirit: the multiplication in the world of impure and evil offspring of the flesh retards the victory of the Light. One can use women, but only for sensual pleasure, not for offspring. Cf. *De mor. Manich.* 2.18.65 ML 32.1372 f.; *De haer.* 46 ML 42.34.

The Priscillianists also taught that marriage was evil and the procreation of children worthy of condemnation. Cf. *De haer.* 70 ML 42.44. See G. Combes, *Oeuvres de saint Augustin* 2.543 n. 1; Pereira, *La doctrine du mariage* 32 ff. For a study of the religion of the Manichees, see Burkitt, *Religion of the Manichees*.

30. It was Jovinian who put marriage on a par with virginity. Jerome in his *Adversus Jovinianum* tells us that he was a monk who gave up the religious life and who, when he was about 35, thought of leading a happier life to compensate for the austerities of the clois-

ter. Augustine is more charitable: "For some years," he says, "there lived at Rome a certain Jovinian who persuaded religious to marry. He did not mean to seduce anyone to enter marriage. He simply thought that persons consecrated by the vow of virginity did not have any more merit before God than those living in marriage." Cf. *De pec. merit. et remis.* 3.7.13 ML 44.193. St. Jerome wrote his *Adversus Jovinianum* in refutation of this heresy. But he praised virginity so highly that marriage seemed of little value in comparison with it. The followers of Jovinian accused Jerome of going over to the side of the Manicheans.

In *De bono conjugali* (401) Augustine strikes a happy medium between the excess of the Manicheans and that of the Jovinianists. Against the former he shows that marriage is the basis of society and that its great dignity and importance consists in three basic facts: the procreation of children (*proles*), the pact of fidelity and of love (*fides*), and the sacramental character (*sacramentum*). The procreation of children renovates society and is a remedy for concupiscence. The pact of fidelity leaves no place for polygamy, demands that marriage be monogamous, and draws the couple closer in love of each other. The sacrament sanctifies conjugal love and gives it the divine guarantee of eternity. In this way Augustine disproves the false teaching of the Manicheans.

As regards the error of Jovinian, Augustine shows that virginity is more excellent than marriage. This is the teaching of Christ and of St. Paul. But it is wrong to believe, as do the Manicheans, that it suffices to be a virgin in order to be more excellent than a married person. One often finds more virtue in the home than in the cloister. It is not a question of individuals but of two states in life. It is clear that in itself virginity is greater. In marriage the spouses try to please one another; the virgin is content to please only God. The virgin also leads her life on a superior plane and goes to God in a more direct manner. See G. Combes, *Oeuvres* 2.19–23, 545 n. 2. See also Hugo, *St. Augustine on Nature* 106–36.

31. Rom. 14.21.

32. The Manichean was obliged to abstain entirely from meat and from wine. Animals and wine were considered creatures of the devil and were consequently essentially unclean. But he was permitted such beverages as *mulsum*, *caroenum passum et nonnullorum pomorum*

expressos succos . . . succum hordei. Cf. *De mor. Man.* 13.29; 16.46 ML 32.1357, 1365. *Mulsum* very likely was a wine made from honey, *caroenum* a raisin wine, and *succus hordei* a drink similar to beer. The elect only were bound strictly to these obligations. See Bardy, "Manichéisme," DTC 9.2.1879. The Priscillianists abstained from meat and even from vegetables cooked with meat, not as a mortification but because they looked upon meat as an unclean food. Cf. *De haer.* 70 ML 42.44. The Catholic stand on meats and foods is stated by St. Paul in these words, which have the ring of a proverb: *All things are clean to the clean* (Titus 1.15), that is, all food, since it comes from God, is clean by its very nature. St. Paul has in mind here those Jews who insisted upon the ancient Mosaic law concerning clean and unclean meats. Certain animal foods were unclean in the Old Law not because they were so by nature but because of a symbolical significance. Some have taken these words as an excuse for sin, namely, that for the clean nothing can be unclean, not even sin, a sense which St. Paul did not mean at all. The Fathers were quick to realize the axiomatic value of these words of Paul and invoked them in many situations and for a great variety of problems and disputes. See Plumpe, "Omnia munda mundis" 509–23.

33. 1 Tim. 4.4.

34. Jovinian wrote a brochure of propaganda in which he expressed his ideas and which Pope Siricius (384–98) called *conscriptio temeraria* and *scriptura horrifica* (cf. Mansi, *Concil.* 3.663). He also wrote a number of tracts or *commentarioli* in justification of his views. Both these works were lost. But those who have refuted them, Jerome, Ambrose, Pope Siricius, Augustine, Vincent of Lerins, have quoted a number of passages from them which help us to reconstruct their contents. Besides the error concerning marriage which we saw above (n. 30) Jovinian taught (1) that there is no difference, from the point of view of the perfection of the soul, between a meal which one takes and thanks God for and fasting which one imposes on oneself to please God; (2) that there will be an equal recompense in heaven for all those who have been faithful to the grace of baptism; (3) that all sins are equally grave; (4) that Mary conceived miraculously through the operation of the Holy Spirit but lost her virginity through childbirth; (5) that those who have received baptism with a full faith cannot sin anymore.

What Jovinian was really teaching was salvation by faith alone, without works. All that is necessary is to receive baptism with a full faith. The rest—marriage, virginity, fasting, and any other good work—mattered little, since one was no better than the other in merit, and since it was really not necessary to perform them to be saved. Baptism and a full faith made it impossible for a person to fall away. This idea of salvation through faith and baptism only influenced many minds towards the end of the fourth century, and Augustine had to oppose it vigorously in *De fide et operibus* (n. 4 above). Pope Siricius condemned the teachings of Jovinian in a Roman synod in the year 390. See Combes, *Oeuvres de saint Augustin* 545, n. 2; Tixeront, *History* 2.243–46.

35. Matt. 7.6.

36. Matt. 18.18.

37. The Donatist schism began in Africa in 311 during the persecution of Diocletian and flourished until the Conference at Carthage in 411. In 312, 70 bishops of Numidia had gathered together in Carthage and unjustly deposed Cecilian, bishop of Carthage. One of the charges brought against him was that his ordination was not valid because he had been ordained by a *traditor*, i.e. by one who had betrayed the sacred books into the hands of pagan persecutors. They put in his place a certain Majorinus, who was succeeded by Donatus the Great, from whom the schism very likely took its name. In the Conference of 411 between the Catholics and the Donatists, Augustine proved the innocence of Cecilian and of his consecrator, Felix of Aptunga.

The Donatists separated themselves from the Catholic Church under the pretext that sinners could not belong to the true Church of Christ. Augustine, on the other hand, shows that the true Church, the Catholic Church, is a mixed society, in other words, a society of saints and sinners: *permixta ecclesia, corpus Christi mixtum* (cf. *In Joan. tract.* 27.11 ML 35.1621; *De doct. christ.* 3.45 ML 34.82). The Scriptures supply Augustine with his most potent arguments against the Donatists: the Church is the threshing floor on which chaff and grain are mixed together, the field of wheat and cockle which must not be separated until the harvest, i.e. until the end of the world. Other images from the Bible which he uses to show that sinners are a part of the Church are the ark of Noe, which contained clean and unclean animals, the miraculous draught of good and bad fishes, and the image of the sheep and the goats. See Batiffol, *Catholicisme* 251–68; Grabowski, "Sinners and the Mystical Body," *Theol. Studies* 8 (1947) 619–32; Willis, *St. Augustine and the Donatist Controversy* 6 ff.

38. See n. 37 above.

39. See ibid.

40. See ibid.

41. Cyprian had already said that good Christians should not leave the Church under the pretext that there are bad Christians in the Church. Cf. *Ep. synod. de lapsis* 3 ML 3.884. Augustine goes furthur and shows that sinners in the Church cannot harm the good as long as the good do not consent to the evil deeds of the bad. The treatise *Contra epistulam Parmeniani*, which Augustine wrote in 400, deals with this very question. Cf. *Retract.* 2.17 CSEL 36.151.

42. Matt. 7.6.

43. If a catechumen desired to complete his initiation and receive baptism, he handed in his name to the authorities. He then underwent an examination to determine whether he was worthy. If the examination was favorable, his name was written in the register of the Church and from then on he was called an *electus* or *competens*, i.e. one chosen for, or one seeking admission to, baptism. The name was given in usually at the beginning of Lent, so that the 40 days of Lent were a time of intense preparation for baptism. During this time the candidate was obliged to fast, to abstain, to practice continence if he was married, and to be present frequently at church in order to undergo exorcisms and hear instructions. This was the immediate preparation for baptism, and one of its chief purposes was to instruct and purify the candidate for a worthy reception of this great sacrament. See Duchesne, *Christian Worship* 293; Bareille, "Catéchuménat," DTC 2.2.1976, 1977.

44. Even in the case of danger of death the usual questions had to be asked and answered: *Subito periculo mortis incipit (homo) perturbari et poscit baptismum, quem tanta festinatione accipit, ut necessariam interrogationem paucorum verborum vix periculi tempus admittat* (*De bapt.* 1.13.21 CSEL 51.165). These questions concerned the moral conversion of the person to be baptized and also the basic truths of the faith as contained in the Creed, or *symbolum*, which at that time played an important role in the ceremony of baptism and which in

normal circumstances the candidate for baptism was required to learn and recite by heart. Where a person was deprived of the use of reason, the renunciation of sin and the confession of faith were made by sponsors or witnesses, as in the case of infants. Augustine followed the principle that it was much better to give than to deny the sacrament: *multo satius est nolenti dare quam volenti negare* (*De conj. adult.* 1.26.33 CSEL 41.380). See Busch, *De initiatione christiana* 115.

45. One of the principal purposes of the immediate preparation for baptism was the instruction of the candidates. Previous to his admission into the *competentes*, the catechumen, in spite of the fact that he did receive some instruction, nevertheless was ignorant of many important facts of Catholic faith and life. He was not as yet initiated into the sacred mysteries, as, e.g., the sacraments, the Creed, the Lord's Prayer, and the great dogmas of the Trinity, the Incarnation, the Redemption, etc. It was necessary, therefore, to complete the education of the catechumen in regard to both faith and morals, and this, of course, was the purpose of these instructions. Examples of such instructions are the sermons of Augustine *ad competentes* and the *Procatechesis* and *Catechesis* 1 of St. Cyril of Jerusalem. See Bareille, "Catéchuménat" 2.2.1979–81.

46. The word used is *catechizare*, derived from *katēchein* = "to teach, to inform by word of mouth." Tertullian was the first Latin writer to use *catechizare* in the meaning of "instruct orally" in the Christian faith. Cf. *De cor. mil.* 9: *Quem Petrus catechizat*. The word *catechismus* (instruction) is first found in Augustine, *De fide et op.* 9.14, 13.19 CSEL 41.51, 59. See Christopher, *Augustine: First Catechetical Instruction* 93 n. 4.

47. Some have thought that there were several classes of catechumens, but F. X. Funk (*Theol. Quartalschr.* 65 [1883] 41–77; 71 [1889] 434–43) has shown conclusively that there was only one. Duchesne, *Christian Worship* 293, follows Funk. See also Gatterer, *Katechetik* 22 ff. The Church required that her converts submit to four periods of instruction, but in this system there was really only one class of catechumens. Those who had acquired the right to be called Christians formed the largest class and went through the longest period of instruction. The *accedentes*, candidates for admission to the catechumenate, constituted another class. The *competentes* formed a third class, while the newly baptized, the *neophyti*, who continued to

receive instructions during the octave of Easter, constituted a fourth. See Christopher, ACW 2.3–4.

48. The preparation for baptism consisted of a series of exercises and instructions during the season of Lent. The meetings for this purpose were called "scrutinies." As the name suggests, the scrutinies were intended to test the preparation of the candidates, and especially to present them to the faithful, who, if the occasion arose, could protest against the admission of anyone who might be unworthy. At the first scrutiny the candidates gave in their names. The third scrutiny was of special importance, for it was then that the candidates were officially instructed in the Gospel, the Creed, and the Lord's Prayer. This was the ceremony at Rome. In Africa the instructions at this stage were limited to the Creed and the Our Father, and the ceremony was called the *traditio symboli* and the *traditio* of the *Pater*. See Duchesne, *Christian Worship* 298 ff.; Kelly, *Early Christian Creeds* 31–36.

49. Col. 3.9.

50. Matt. 9.16 f.

51. The catechumenate was an institution of the early Church which had as its object the preparation of converts for baptism. It was a period during which converts learned and put into practice their essential duties in regard to belief and conduct. Entrance into the catechumenate was accompanied by ceremonies of insufflation, signing with the cross on the forehead, and administering of salt. The ceremonies differed in different places. Catechumens were regarded as Christians and were admitted to religious assemblies, but not to the Eucharistic liturgy properly so called. They were assigned a special place in the church and were dismissed before the beginning of the holy mysteries. According to the decrees of the Council of Elvira (A.D. 303—Mansi 2.5–19), the catechumenate lasted in ordinary cases for two years. However, if they so desired, catechumens could remain in their probationary stage as long as they liked. The Emperors Constantine and Constantius, in the fourth century, remained catechumens until they were at the point of death. See Duchesne, *Christian Worship* 292, 295–97; Bareille, "Catéchuménat" 2.2.1968 ff.

52. Immediately after baptism the catechumen received the sacraments of confirmation and of the Holy Eucharist. These three

sacraments, the sacraments of initiation, all formed a part of the solemn ceremony of baptism.

53. 1 Cor. 11.29.

54. Ps. 48(47).2.

55. I have translated the word *vinculum* (bond, fetter, tie) as "contract." When Augustine speaks of marriage, he does not call it specifically a contract. It is true, he uses the term in his *De diversis quaestionibus ad Simplicianum* 2.16 ML 40.120. However, the word in this case has the meaning more of a debt owed rather than an agreement or consent made, or, in other words, a contract. Although we do not find in Augustine the contract-sacrament theory of marriage in the same form as we have it today, nevertheless, by his teaching on the *fides* and the *sacramentum*, he has done much to bring to light these two elements of marriage, i.e. contract and sacrament. See Serrier, *De quelques recherches* 2.76–95; Kuiters, "Augustin et l'indissolubilité" 5–11.

56. Augustine's use of the word "sacrament" in relation to marriage has various meanings. The following are the principal ones. (1) He uses it in the sense of a mysterious character or property of marriage, which he calls simply the "sacrament of marriage," *sacramentum nuptiarum* (*De pec. orig.* 37.42 CSEL 42.200). (2) Sacrament means a figure, a sign, a symbol: *Sicut ergo sacramentum pluralium nuptiarum illius temporis significavit futuram multitudinem Deo subjectam in terrenis omnibus gentibus, sic sacramentum nuptiarum singularum nostri temporis significat unitatem omnium nostrum subjectam Deo futuram in una coelesti civitate* (*De bono conj.* 18.21 CSEL 41.215). (3) It is a seal, a *sigillum*. In the New Law a man cannot divorce his wife for any reason. One could not understand such severity if the conjugal bond were not strengthened by a seal (*sacramentum*) of something superior to man's mortal condition (cf. *De bono conj.* 7.7 CSEL 41.197). (4) It means an indissoluble bond: *sacramentum vero, quod nec separati nec adulterati amittunt, conjuges concorditer casteque custodiant* (*De nupt. et concup.* 1.17 CSEL 42.231). See Ladomérszky, *Augustin, docteur du mariage* 116–21; Christopher, ACW 2.108 n. 87.

Augustine sees in the sacrament of marriage a sacred sign. It is thus that he considers marriage as a figure, a symbol, a sign. Christian marriage is a sacred symbol of the union between Christ and the

Church. But one does not find in him any clear allusion to marriage as a sacrament instituted by Christ. Nor does he ever speak explicitly of the grace connected with this sacrament. Yet, if we consider the whole of Augustine's doctrine concerning the sacraments of the New Law, which, according to him, all confer the grace they signify, we can say that marriage also produces grace, since he attributes to it the sanctity of a sacrament. See Ladomérszky, ibid. 122–31; Pereira, *La doctrine du mariage* 199–223.

57. Augustine does not think of marriage as indissoluble in itself. Christian marriage is indissoluble for him because it is a symbol, a sensible sign of the inseparable union of Christ with the Church. Cf. *De nupt. et concup.* 1.10 CSEL 42.222; *De bono conj.* 7.7 ML 40.378. Christian husband and wife are morally obligated to reproduce in themselves the union of Christ and his Church: "Husbands, love your wives, just as Christ also loved the Church" (Eph. 5.25). Anyone who breaks the bond is condemned as an adulterer, not by the law of the world but by the law of the gospel. Cf. *De nupt. et concup.* 1.10 CSEL 42.223. Nothing can separate the Christian couple, neither dismissal because of fornication, nor simple separation, nor sterility, nor the vow of continence; only death can break the bond. Cf. *De bono conj.* 24.32 CSEL 41.227. For Augustine, Christian marriage is a sacrament, and this is the fundamental reason why it is indissoluble. See Ladomérszky, *Augustin, docteur du mariage* 140–52; Kuiters, *Augustin et l'indissolubilité* 5–11.

58. Cf. Plutarch, *Cat. min.*, c. 25.

59. The distinction between mortal and venial sin is very clear and precise in Augustine. Up to his time there was a vague notion concerning this matter even amongst the better authors. Mortal sins he calls *crimina*, *letalia*, *mortifera;* these separate one from the kingdom of God. Venial sins are *peccata quotidiana*, *levia*, *parva*, etc.; these are compatible with grace and the right to heaven. See Portalié, "Augustin" 1.2.2440 ff.; Mausbach, *Die Ethik* 1.230–41; Durkin, *Theological Distinction of Sins* 12–17.

60. *Regula fidei—kanōn tēs pisteōs*—is the term used by the ancients for the profession of faith made by the candidate for baptism. For other passages in which Augustine uses *regula fidei*-creed (*symbolum*), see Mohrmann, *Die altchristliche Sondersprache* 142. For a his-

tory of the African Creed, see Badcock, "Le Credo primitif d'Afrique" 3–9. Cf. Arand, ACW 3.131 n. 180.

61. Every human act must be performed with the right intention if it is to be good. All our moral actions depend on the motive for their moral goodness: *non actibus, sed finibus pensantur officia* (*Cont. Jul.* 4.3.26 ML 44.751). It is the intention, not the objective goodness of an act, which determines the morality of an act: *Nec faciunt bonos vel malos mores, nisi boni vel mali amores* (*Ep.* 155.4.13 ML 33.672). The motive of which Augustine speaks is that of supernatural charity, that charity which is produced in us by the grace of Christ. Thus, to avoid sin in our acts two essential conditions are required: (1) to avoid that which is bad in itself; (2) to avoid it out of love for God. It is necessary, in a word, in order to avoid sin, to know and to practice the doctrine of Christ.

Baius was of the opinion that according to Augustine it was impossible to do the least good without charity and that, consequently, the virtues of the pagans are vices and all their actions sins. When Augustine condemns the virtues of the pagans, he does not condemn their objective or material goodness; he does not condemn the act considered in itself, but the act taken in the concrete. Thus, almsgiving considered in itself is clearly a good act: *ipsa (misericordia) per se ipsam naturali compassione opus est bonum* (*Cont. Jul.* 4.3.31 ML 44.754). What he condemns is the real act in so far as it proceeds from a bad will and is motivated by a bad intention. But he never condemns as bad, even among pagans, almsgiving, patience, devotion to one's country, when he considers them apart from the intention of the agent. The defect of the virtues of the pagans, according to Augustine, is that, for the most part, they are not directed to God, to their supernatural end. See Combes, *La charité* 269–83; Martin, *Saint Augustin* 218–23; Wang, *Saint Augustin et les vertus des païens.*

62. E. Portalié in his DTC article on Augustine (1.2.2432) says that no one knew better than Augustine the intimate connection between faith and morals. With the exception of a few minor works, practically all of his many writings are dogmatic. Yet, in all these writings he is always conscious of the moral value of the dogmas which he treats.

63. The term "faithful" (*fidelis*) was reserved for those who were baptized. "Christian" (*christianus*), a more general term, in-

cluded all those who were to be members of the Church, as well as those who were baptized. Thus catechumens were called Christians. See Augustine, *In Joan. tract.* 44.2 ML 35.1714: *Interroga hominem: Christianus es? respondet tibi: non sum, si paganus est aut Judaeus. Si autem dixerit: sum, adhuc quaeris ab eo: catechumenus an fidelis?* See Quasten, *Monumenta eucharistica* 91 n. 1.

64. See n. 47 above. During the octave of Easter the newly baptized (*neophyti, illuminati*) received instructions on the sacraments which they had just received, i.e. baptism, confirmation, and the Eucharist. Examples of such instructions are the *Catecheses mystagogicae* of Cyril of Jerusalem, and the *De mysteriis* and the *De sacramentis* of Ambrose. See Quasten, *Monumenta* 2 ff.

65. Acts 2.37 f.

66. Eph. 4.28.

67. Acts 2.38–41.

68. See n. 45 above.

69. Acts 8.37.

70. In the actual baptism ceremony the candidate was required to recite the Creed before all present: *audientibus omnibus* (*Serm.* 58.1.1 ML 38.393). Then followed the interrogations: Do you renounce the world and the devil? Do you believe in the Father and the Son and the Holy Spirit? The interrogations were not limited to the dogma of the Trinity but included all the articles of the Creed. This whole procedure was known as professing the faith, *professio fidei.* See Gendreau, *Augustini doctrina de baptismo* 32 ff.; de Puniet, "Baptême" 2.1.315–17; Kelly, *Early Christian Creeds* 31–36.

71. See n. 44 above.

72. The word used is *catechismus,* which I have here translated as "preach." See n. 46 above.

73. In order that a man be born, he must be born of man and woman; in like manner, in order that a man become a member of the Body of Christ, he must be reborn of God and the Church. Cf. *Serm.* 121.4 ML 38.680. To be born of God is to begin a new life by the grace and justification of which He is the author. Cf. *Serm.* 119.4 ML 38.674. To be born of the Church is to receive and begin this new life in baptism, which has been entrusted to the Church as the sacrament of regeneration. Cf. *De pec. merit. et remis.* 2.27.43 CSEL 60.114. Hence, all who have received this sacrament in the Church

are said "to have been regenerated in Christ and born from above." Cf. *Sermo* 34.3.6 ML 38.211. They have become new men (*Enar. in ps.* 75.15 ML 36.966), renovated by baptism (*Ep.* 190.5.16 CSEL 57.152), and have put on Christ (*Ep. ad Gal.* 27 ML 35.2124). These effects produced in the baptized person are concomitant with, and inseparable from, incorporation into the Body of Christ. "When you have been baptized," says Augustine, "then you have been born members" (*Serm.* Denis 25 Morin, *Aug. serm.* 164). Incorporation into the Body of Christ cannot be had except by baptism or martyrdom in behalf of Christ. Cf. *De anima et ejus orig.* 1.9.10 ML 44.480. In fact, the sacrament of baptism is so closely linked with incorporation into the Body of Christ that Augustine speaks here of baptism as the actual incorporation into the Body of Christ, whereas it is the effect of baptism rather than the sacrament which causes that incorporation. See Grabowski, "Augustine and the Mystical Body" 84 ff.; idem, *The Church* 26 ff.

74. The Holy Spirit is often referred to in Scripture as the "gift" of God (Jn 4.10; Acts 2.38 and 8.20). Cf. Augustine, *De cat. rud.* 27.55 ML 40.348: *Quam non implet, nisi qui donum acceperit Spiritum Sanctum*"; *Conf.* 13.19 CSEL 33.351: *Cur ergo tantum de Spiritu tuo dictum est hoc . . . de quo solo dictum est, quod sit donum tuum.* This gift of God, this love eternal and infinitely delectable, is given to us and His charity is diffused in our hearts. This diffusion makes ours the charity of God, which in us, however, is not the substantial and subsisting charity of the Trinity but a communication of divine ardor and fire. Cf. *De trin.* 15.19.37 ML 42.1086. See Grabowski, "The Role of Charity" 34 ff.; Christopher, ACW 2.132 n. 222.

75. Christ, says Augustine, can be understood, according to the Scriptures, in a threefold manner. First, He is represented as true God, possessing equality of nature and eternity with God the Father. In this view of Christ, we prescind from any consideration of His human nature. Second, He is God made man in the Incarnation. Since He possesses both natures, the human and the divine, He is Mediator and Head of the Church. Third, Christ is to be considered not as an individual but in His fulness, i.e. with the whole Church, with all the members, of whom He is the Head, as constituting one unit, one whole, one person, as it were. Cf. *Serm.* 341.1.1 ML 39.1493. It is in this third way that Augustine very often considers

both Christ in His relation to the Church, and the Church inasmuch as she is intimately and inseparably joined to Christ. He expresses this whole relation between Christ and the Church, in so far as Christ Himself is concerned, by calling Christ "the Head of the Church." See Grabowski, "Augustine and the Mystical Body" 74 ff.; idem, *The Church* 10 ff.

76. 1 Cor. 2.2.

77. 1 Cor. 4.15.

78. 1 Cor. 14.16.

79. 1 Cor. 15.3 f.

80. Rom. 6.6.

81. Gal 6.14.

82. 1 Peter 4.1 f.

83. Matt. 2.37–39.

84. 1 John 4.20.

85. 1 John 2.15.

86. When speaking of baptism, its nature and its effects, the Fathers often describe it by the figures of baptism which exist in the Old Testament. One of these is the figure of the Red Sea. The deliverance of the Jews and the drowning of the Egyptians represents the deliverance of the soul from its sins by the waters of baptism and the victory over her enemies. See Quasten, *Monumenta* 73 n. 2; 119 n. 4; Dölger, "Der Durchzug" 63–69.

87. See n. 48 above. A few weeks before baptism the *competentes* were given instructions on the Creed and on the Lord's Prayer. First they were taught the Creed. It was explained to them article by article and they were required to learn it by heart, since they would recite it in a solemn manner on the day of their baptism. Then followed the instructions on the Lord's Prayer. The same procedure was followed here as in the Creed. This was the so-called *traditio* and *redditio symboli* and the *traditio* and *redditio orationis dominicae*. The *traditio symboli*, i.e. the giving of the Creed to the *competentes*, was the high point of the catechumenate. The *redditio symboli*, i.e. the reciting of the Creed on the day of baptism, was the official conclusion of the catechumenate and also the final proof of the worthiness of the candidate to receive baptism. See Busch, *De initiatione christiana* 76–82; Kelly, *Early Christian Creeds* 31–36; Eichenseer, *Das Symbolum apostolicum* 134–36.

88. Exod. 12.7 ff.

89. Act 2.39.

90. Augustine regarded the Epistle to the Hebrews as canonical. Cf. *De pecc. mer. et remis.* 1.50 ML 44.137: *ad Hebraeos . . . epistola quamquam nonnullis incerta sit . . . magis . . . me movet auctoritas ecclesiarum orientalium, quae hanc etiam in canonicis habent.* However, he remained uncertain as to the Pauline authorship of the epistle. Cf. *De civ. Dei* 16.22 CSEL 40^2.164. See Prat, *Theology of Saint Paul* 1.476.

91. Heb. 6.1 f.

92. Exod. 20.3–5.

93. We do not find among Christian writers before Augustine any sermon, catechesis, or treatise on the Decalogue. Origen has a homily (*Hom. 8 in Exod.*) on the First Commandment, but this is a sermon against idolatry rather than a treatment of the Decalogue. Augustine was the first to use the Decalogue as a norm for Christian moral instruction. Until then this norm was rather the twofold commandment of love. It is not that the Decalogue was disregarded, but it did not have a dominant place in Christian moral instruction until Augustine. He was the first to interpret it in its New Testament or Christian sense and to show that it adequately expresses the Christian moral code. As early as 397, in *Sermon* 9.7 and 13, Augustine began to insist on the importance of the Decalogue. He gives a complete treatment of the subject in his treatise *Contra Faustum*. Here he shows again and again that the Ten Commandments are the basis of all true morality, and that all of them are contained in the two great commandments of love of God and love of neighbor. See Rentschka, *Die Dekalogkatechese* 1 ff., 12 ff., 21 ff.; Christopher, ACW 2.95 n. 10, 102 n. 51, 138 n. 271.

94. Exod. 20.12 ff.

95. See n. 2 above.

96. See n. 1 above.

97. 2 Cor. 6.16.

98. 1 Cor. 6.15.

99. 1 Cor. 6.9 f.

100. 1 Cor. 6.11.

101. See n. 4 above.

102. Matt. 3.7 f.

103. Luke 3.14.

104. Luke 3.12 f.

105. See n. 46 above.

106. Matt. 19.16–21.

107. See n. 62 above.

108. Rom. 3.8.

109. Rom. 5.20

110. Ps. 120.2.

111. Rom. 5.5.

112. By promulgating the law, God foresaw the acts of disobedience which it would occasion, but He foresaw at the same time the way in which He would turn to account these very faults: by humbling the sinner, by awakening his conscience, by convincing him of his impotence, and by making him desire divine aid. In this way God brings good out of evil. But when He permits it in view of the good which results from it, Scripture usually says that He wishes and orders it. Thus St. Paul says that "the law entered in, *in order* that sin might abound; . . . *so that* grace might reign by justice unto life eternal" (Rom. 5.20 f.). See Prat, *Theology of Saint Paul* 1.183 ff.; Gilson, *Introduction* 199 ff.

113. Ps. 16(15).4.

114. Rom. 3.28; Gal. 2.16.

115. St. Paul expresses man's justification by faith in two ways: "a man is not justified by works of the law, but through faith in Jesus Christ" (Gal. 2.16); "a man is justified by faith without the works of the law" (Rom. 3.28). That it is a question here of first justification, of passing from the state of sin to that of justice, is shown clearly from the context in both cases. In the Epistle to the Romans, Paul devotes three chapters to proving that all persons reduced to their own strength or to the resources of the law only are sinners; now he inquires whence comes the justice which excludes sin, consequently the first justice. In the Epistle to the Galatians he reminds Peter of the reason which impelled them to embrace the faith; this reason is that justice comes from faith only, i.e., considering the situation, the *first* justice. Paul is not concerned in either case with the part which works play *after* justification. That they are then necessary is evident from his teaching in general, but in the controversy with the Judaizers the question was chiefly that of first justification. The works of the law are neither the cause, nor the necessary condition, nor even,

in themselves, the occasion of this first justification. See Prat, *Theology of Saint Paul* 1.174 ff.

116. The book *De spiritu et littera* (cf. *Retract.* 2.37 CSEL 36.175 ML 44.201–46) was written in answer to a letter of Marcellinus, who wrote to Augustine that he was disturbed by having read in his work *De peccatorum meritis et remissione* that it was possible for man aided by grace to live without sin, but that *de facto* this is not the case. The words *spiritus* and *littera*, which are borrowed from 2 Cor. 3.6, are the equivalent of grace and law. The law by itself is the letter that kills, since without grace it cannot be observed. It is the grace of the Holy Spirit which makes it possible for man to keep the law. Nevertheless, even with grace no man *de facto* is sinless. Augustine wrote this work towards the end of the year 412.

117. Gal. 5.6.

118. 1 Cor. 13.2.

119. Rom. 13.10.

120. 2 Peter 3.11–18.

121. At first sight, St. Paul and St. James seem to contradict each other in their teaching on justification. Paul says that "man is justified by faith without the works of the law" (Rom. 3.28); St. James, "man is justified by works and not by faith only" (James 2.24). But the two apostles are not speaking of the same things. The works which Paul has in mind are those *preceding* faith and justice, those chiefly of the law, which is the object of his discussion with the Judaizers; the works of James are those which *follow* faith and justice, since he is speaking to Christians already in possession of the supernatural life. The justice of which Paul speaks is *first* justice, i.e. a passing from a state of sin to a state of holiness; the justice of James is *second* justice, otherwise known as the increase of justice, the regular development of the Christian life. In short, Paul is thinking of man *before* justification, James *after* justification. The former has in mind a *living* faith, a faith activated by charity; the latter, a faith that may be *dead*, a faith minus charity. The one is speaking to the *unbeliever* and he says to him that without faith he cannot be justified; the other speaks to the *Christian* and he tells him that his conduct must harmonize with his faith, for faith alone is not enough to make him just. See Prat, *Theology of Saint Paul* 1.180 ff.; Tobac, "Le problème de la justification" 797–805; Bergauer, *Der Jakobusbrief* 67–71.

122. James 2.19.
123. Mark 1.24 f.; Matt. 16.16.
124. James 2.14.
125. James 2.20.
126. 1 Cor. 3.11–15.
127. See note 4 above.
128. See note 2 above.
129. 1 Cor. 13.2.
130. James 2.14.
131. 1 Cor. 6.9 f.
132. Gal. 5.19–21.
133. 1 Cor. 6.11.
134. 1 Peter 3.21.
135. Matt. 19.17.
136. Matt. 19.18 f.
137. James 2.17.
138. Matt. 25.41.
139. Matt. 25.44.
140. See note 4 above. The giving of alms played a very important part in the life and teaching of the early Church. St. Cyprian wrote a special treatise on the subject, *De opere et eleemosynis* (ca. 253). In this work he compares the efficacy of almsgiving with that of baptism: *Sicut lavacro aquae salutaris gehennae ignis extinguitur, ita eleemosynis atque operationibus justis delictorum flamma sopitur* (ibid. 2). Cf. Galtier, *L'Église et la rémission des péchés* 47 ff. In subapostolic times the Christians were admonished to give alms from the fruit of their labor and in this way free themselves from the guilt of sin. Cf. *Didache* 4.6 ff.; *Ep. Barnabae* 19.10; Hermas, *Pastor*, *mand.* 2.4–7. See Geoghegan, *Attitude toward Labor* 116, 125, 132. It was necessary, however, in Augustine's time to warn the people against the error of placing too much value on the efficacy of almsgiving as a means of atoning for sins: *Sane cavendum est ne quisquam existimet infanda illa crimina, qualia qui agunt, regnum Dei non possidebunt, quotidie perpetranda, et eleemosynis quotidie redimenda. In melius quippe est vita mutanda, et per eleemosynas de peccatis praeteritis est propitiandus Deus; non ad hoc emendus quodam modo, ut ea semper liceat impune committere. Nemini enim dedit laxamentum peccandi* (Eccli. 15.21), *quamvis*

miserando deleat jam facta peccata, si non satisfactio congrua negligatur (*Enchir.* 70.19 ML 40.265). See Arand, ACW 3.134 n. 234.

141. 1 Cor. 13.3.

142. Ps. 10.6.

143. At the beginning of the fifth century, as we saw above in n. 4, there existed in the Western Church a number of errors which presented salvation as more or less independent of good works, and which denied the eternity of the pains of hell for all the reprobate or, at least, for certain classes of sinners. Augustine refutes the former in the *De civ. Dei* 21.23–27 CSEL 40^2.555 ff., and here in *De fide et op.* 14.21 ff.

As regards the nature and duration of the punishment of the reprobate, Augustine was very firm and positive, at least on those points which pertain to dogma strictly so called. The damned shall suffer a common punishment, the *alienatio a vita Dei* (*Enchir.* 113 ML 40.285), to which will be added a punishment of an inferior kind, one that we would call the pain of sense. The fire of hell is a real and material fire which will torture the damned—men and devils—both in their bodies and in their souls. If angels do not have bodies, this fire will torture them in their spiritual being, *quamvis miris, tamen veris modis* (*De civ. Dei* 21.10 CSEL 40^2.537). These torments will differ according to the degree of guilt of the one condemned. The suffering of children who die without baptism will be *mitissima omnium poena* (*Enchir.* 93 ML 40.275; *De civ. Dei* 21.16 CSEL 40^2.548); but for all, the punishment will certainly be eternal. This is a subject which Augustine treats again and again, precisely because he realized that it met with much opposition. Cf. *Enchir.* 111–13 ML 40.284 ff.; *De civ. Dei* 21.11, 13, 18–27 CSEL 40^2.539, 542, 549–81. He proves the eternity of the pains of hell by Scripture, especially by the texts of the Apocalypse (20.9 f.) and of Matthew (25.41, 46), by the custom of the Church in not praying for the damned, and even tries to justify it by reason. As to the view which admitted periodic interruptions of the pains of hell, he neither favors nor condemns it absolutely: *Poenas damnatorum certis temporum intervallis existiment, si hoc eis placet, aliquatenus mitigari. Quod quidem non ideo confirmo, quoniam non resisto* (*Enchir.* 112 ML 40.285; cf. *De civ. Dei* 21.24 CSEL 40^2.561). See Tixeront, *History* 2.427 ff.; Eger, *Die Eschatologie Augustins* 68–73; Lehaut, *L'Éternité des peines de l'enfer;* Kelly, *Early Christian Doctrines* 484 ff.

144. Matt. 25.46.
145. Gal. 5.6.
146. James 2.14.
147. Augustine gives the same interpretation of these words in *Enchir.* 68.18 ML 40.264 ff.; *De civ. Dei* 21.26 CSEL 40^2.567 ff.; *Enar. in ps.* 29, *serm.* 2.9 ML 36.221 ff.; ibid. *serm.* 80.21 ML 37.1044 f. Augustine's interpretation of this passage of Paul is not a denial of any kind of purification after this life—see n. 161 below—but rather a denial of that opinion which, as we saw above in n. 4, said that all who had the faith and were baptized would be saved, even though they had led evil lives. See Perl, *Drei Bücher* xxiv; Landgraf, "1 Cor. 3.10–17" 148 ff.; Durkin, *Theological Distinction of Sins* 134 ff.
148. 1 Cor. 3.11.
149. Eph. 3.17.
150. Gal. 5.6.
151. James 2.19.
152. Matt. 19.18 f.
153. Matt. 19.21.
154. 1 Cor. 7.32.
155. 1 Cor. 7.33.
156. Gal. 5.6.
157. 1 Cor. 7.15.
158. Augustine treats the Pauline Privilege in *De conjugiis adulterinis* 1.13.14 ff. CSEL 41.361. Here he specifies against Pollentius that St. Paul is speaking of two persons married in infidelity, one of whom is converted to Christianity; that he is not speaking in the name of Christ but in his own name only; that he is not giving a command or an order but only a simple permission. Augustine then studies the character of this permission and arrives at the following conclusions. (1) The Christian partner does not have the right to use this permission except in the case that the non-Christian partner makes married life insupportable by his reproaches, insults, and persecutions. (2) In most cases and for the most part, the reasons or causes which legitimize this permission do not take into consideration beforehand the grave inconveniences which it brings to those who use it. (3) It is more advantageous for the Christian partner to sanctify and to save the non-Christian partner than to separate from him. (4) In any case,

even in the case of separation, the Christian partner has not the right to remarry.

According to the 1983 Code of Canon Law (1143–47), four conditions are required for the Pauline Privilege: (1) the marriage was contracted in infidelity, i.e. between a man and a woman both unbaptized; (2) conversion and baptism of one of the partners; (3) interpellation made to the non-Christian so as to inform him of the fact of conversion and what it means; (4) refusal of the partner to be baptized or to live in peace with the converted partner. The converted partner may enter a new marriage, and from the moment that he does the former marriage no longer exists. But he must marry in the Church. Thus, today the Pauline Privilege is considered a special and exceptional dissolution of the marriage bond. Its purpose is to safeguard, under the conditions stated above, the superior interests of the faith. See Combes, *Oeuvres* 2.547 n. 3; Pereira, *La doctrine du mariage* 141–48.

159. The Latin has *si . . . habebat uxorem tamquam non habens*. Cf. 1 Cor. 7.29 ff.

160. 1 Cor. 7.32.

161. As we saw above in n. 147, Augustine treats this passage of St. Paul in other places also and in these he gives the same interpretation. There does not seem to be any doubt among scholars that Augustine teaches an expiation after death. The precise nature of the expiation is the problem. Some theologians are of the opinion that the purification and expiation after death but before the final judgment is Augustine's expression of the doctrine of purgatory. Cf. *De civ. Dei* 21.13 ML 41.728. What Augustine doubts is not the existence of purgatory but the nature of its punishments. See Eger, *Die Eschatologie Augustins* 37–40; Portalié, "Augustin" 1.2.2447 ff.; Arand, ACW 3.134. Other theologians say that there is not in Augustine any certain or clear teaching on purgatory, that this teaching did not come into existence till much later, about the beginning of the 12th century. However, it seems that Augustine was the first to express in the form of a hypothesis the idea of a purification between death and the last judgment, an idea which would later be developed by theologians into the doctrine of purgatory. See Perl, *Drei Bücher* 191 ff.; Jay, "Augustin et la doctrine du purgatoire" 22 ff., 26 ff.

162. 1 Tim. 1.10 f.

163. Matt. 15.26.

164. Matt. 15.28.

165. Concerning the sin against the Holy Spirit, Augustine says that "in all Sacred Scripture perhaps no greater, no more difficult question can be found" (*Sermo* 71.5, 8 ML 38.449). He has given various explanations of this sin. Here he interprets it as a refusal to believe in Christ. More often, however, he holds that it is the sin of final impenitence, perseverance till death in mortal sin (cf. *Serm.* 71.12, 20 ML 38.455 ff.; *Ep.* 185.11, 49 ML 33.814; *Ep. ad Rom. inchoata expositio* 14 ML 35.2097; *Enchir.* 83 ML 40.272). See Mangenot, "Blasphème," DTC 2.1.910–16; Lagrange, *Évangile selon saint Matthieu* 244 ff.

166. Gal 5.6.

167. 1 Tim. 1.10 f.

168. Cf. Matt. 22.2 f.

169. See n. 37 above.

170. Matt. 22.10.

171. Matt. 13.39.

172. Matt. 10.11.

173. Matt. 25.15 f.

174. 1 Cor. 6.15

175. Cf. James 2.17.

176. In the writings of Augustine we find references to a superior and inferior order in the clerical state: *Neque enim de presbyteris aut diaconis aut inferioris ordinis clericis, sed de collegis* (*episcopis*) *agebatur* (*Ep.* 43.3, 7 CSEL 34^2.90). To the superior order belong bishops, presbyters, and deacons. To the inferior order belong subdeacon, lector, and acolyte. For the subdiaconate ordination is necessary. Cf. *Ep.* 63.1 CSEL 34^2.226. The office of the lector is to read publicly the canonical Scriptures. Cf. *Ep.* 64.3 CSEL 34^2.231. In a few passages Augustine mentions one acolyte who has the duty of forwarding letters. Cf. *Ep.* 191 CSEL 57^4.163; *Ep.* 193 CSEL 57^4.168.

When Augustine gives the clerical orders of the higher rank, he either descends from the highest to the lower ones (bishops, presbyters, and deacons) or, inversely, he gradually ascends from the lowest to the higher ones. Cf. *Serm.* 356.91 ML 39. 1578. The presbyterate, conferred by specific ordination, ranks below the episcopal office. Augustine tells us that he was made presbyter and that through this grade he arrived at the episcopacy: *presbyter factus sum, et per hunc gradum perveni ad episcopatum* (*Serm.* 355.1, 2 ML 39.1569). Although in a lower order than the episcopacy, the presbyter and the episcopacy had some offices in common, for the presbyter also "ministers the sacrament and the word of God to the people" (*Ep.* 21.3 CSEL 33.51). See Grabowski, *The Church* 104.

177. Matt. 4.19.

178. There is scarcely an aspect of Roman culture that Augustine criticizes more than the theater. He seldom speaks of it without condemning it. He calls it *foedus* (*De civ. Dei* 6.7.74); *turpis* (ibid. 2.4.17; *Serm.* 198.3); *dedecorus* (*Ep.* 138.14); *ludibris* (*De civ. Dei* 6.9.45); *obscoenus* (ibid. 2.4.25). It would be vain to look for any greater denunciation by Augustine than that which he gives in the *City of God* 2.27.16, where he speaks of the theater as *talium numinum placatio petulantissima, impurissima, impudentissima, nequissima, immundissima.* Obviously, for Augustine the profession of the actor, no less than that of the prostitute, was infamous and evil. Consequently, such persons could not be permitted to be baptized unless they were willing to give up their profession. See Weismann, *Kirche und Schauspiele* 151 ff.

179. See n. 2 above.

180. Gal. 5.21. Augustine accepts and expounds the sins mentioned by St. Paul as depriving one of the kingdom of God. These sins destroy the spiritual life of the soul and at the same time divest it of living membership in the corporate life of the Body of Christ. See Grabowski, "Sinners and the Mystical Body" 618.

181. Cf. 1 Cor. 6.10.

182. See n. 2 above. It is difficult to imagine the hold which the public games had on the people of the ancient world. Among the ancients there was less home life and less intimacy with relatives and friends than in the world today. Thus, without the pleasures of the theater and of the circus life seemed rather empty. At Rome, e.g., in the time of Marcus Aurelius, the 135 days that were given over to the public games were for the people the best part of the year; the rest of the year was lived in happy memory of past holidays or looking forward to the ones to come. One of the most bitter complaints of the pagans against the Christians was that the latter condemned these

very spectacles which they enjoyed so much and to which they felt they had a right. For these reasons, even the Christian emperors were always very careful to respect the desires and feelings of the people in this matter. This explains why these games remained in existence even as late as the end of the fourth century.

The above reasons also explain why Augustine, as also the other Fathers of the fourth century, were rather reserved in their criticism of such spectacles. As regards Augustine himself, perhaps another reason why he seldom criticizes the games is because he had no interest in them. Nevertheless, there are times when he does express his disapproval and his horror, as, e.g., when he speaks of the gladiatorial fights as this *licentiosa crudelitas* (*Serm.* 20.3), and of the amphitheatre as *amphitheatrum crudelium et funestorum ludorum* (*Conf.* 6.13). See Boissier, *La fin du paganisme* 1.80–82; 2.168–75; Fliche-Martin, *Histoire de l'église* 3.513–18; 4.15–30; Weismann, *Kirche und Schauspiele* 155, 158.

183. Gal. 5.21. Bishops are the head of each church. Their task is to rule. They are the *praepositi* who preside over the Church. Cf. *De civ. Dei* 20.9, 2 ML 41.673. They are the *rectores* who are compared to Noe steering his ark, because they, as it were, govern the course of the Church. Cf. *Enar. in ps.* 132.5 ML 37. 1731. They are the *custodes* and *pastores* who guide and watch over the faithful. Cf. *Enar. in ps.* 126.3 ML 37.1669. They have, therefore, an *episcopalis auctoritas* (*Ep.* 186.2 ML 33.816) to which belongs the *praepositura*, *gubernatio*, *praeesse*, *regere*, *superintendere* in the Church. All these are terms proper to Augustine which he uses in one form or other to designate the authority of the bishop. Moreover, the bishops are also "doctors" who not only teach the people but also defend the traditional deposit of doctrine against those who contradict it and try to ensnare the faithful. Cf. *Ep.* 186.2 ML 33.816; *Enar. in ps.* 123.3 ML 37.1669; *Serm.* 94 ML 38.580. See Grabowski, *The Church* 108.

184. See n. 140 above.

185. In the ancient Church those sins were mortal, *ad mortem*, *mortalia*, *capitalia*, which were punished with excommunication, and which in ordinary circumstances had to be expiated by public penance. Precisely which sins these were is very hard to say. In general, Augustine puts in this class all those sins which offend against the Decalogue or which St. Paul mentions as excluding from the king-

dom of God (1 Cor. 6.9–11; Gal. 5.19–21). He gives examples of such sins in *Serm.* 56.8, 12 ML 38.382; *De cat. rud.* 25.48 ML 40.343. See Galtier, *De poenitentia* 142, 202 ff.; Poschmann, *Augustini textus selecti de poenitentia* 14 n. 1; La Bonnardière, "Pénitence et réconciliation" 256–58.

186. The excommunication reserved for sins *ad mortem* was exclusion from the Eucharist, or separation from the Body of Christ. This excommunication and the reconciliation afterwards were a part of that penance known as public. Cf. Augustine, *Serm.* 351.4, 7 ML 39.1542 f.; *Ep.* 265.7 CSEL 57.645; *Serm.* 56.8, 12 ML 38.382 f. However, exclusion from the Eucharist was not the distinguishing mark of the public penitent. The Fathers complained of many who did not receive the Eucharist but who did not belong to the ranks of public penitents. Cf. Ambrose, *De poenit.* 2.9, 89 ML 16.539; Augustine, *De civ. Dei* 20.9 CSEL 40^2.451; John Chrysostom, *In Ephes. hom.* 3.4, 5 MG 62.29, 30. Those were public penitents who were assigned a special place in church apart from the rest of the faithful, and who received an imposition of hands special to themselves. Moreover, they received their penance from the priest, which they were obliged to perform, in the place assigned to them, for the length of time determined by him. See Galtier, *De poenitentia* 181 ff.; Poschmann, *Augustini textus selecti de poenitentia* 6 n. 1.

187. Augustine calls public penance *poenitentia humilior*, as here in this place: *donec poenitentia humiliore sanentur; humillima* (*Ep.* 153.3, 7 ML 33.656); *luctuosa et lamentabilis* (*De div. quaest.* 83.26 ML 40.18); *maior et insignior* (*Ep.* 151.9 ML 33.650); *gravior atque luctuosior* (*Serm.* 352.3, 8 ML 39.1558); *poenitentia quae instituta est in ecclesia* (*Serm.* 352.3, 9 ML 39.1559); *poenitentia qualis agitur in ecclesia* (*Serm.* 392.3, 3 ML 39.1711). Those who perform this type of penance are *poenitentes* properly so called, *qui proprie poenitentes vocantur* (*De fide et op.* 26.48 CSEL 41.94; *Ep.* 265.7 CSEL 57.645; *Serm.* 352.3, 8 ML 39.1558). Occasionally this type of penance was called *publica* by the ancients. For example, the Council of Toledo (400) defines a penitent thus: *Poenitenten eum qui . . . publicam poenitentiam gerens divino fuerit reconciliatus altario* (can. 2, Mansi 3.999). The penance imposed upon the Emperor Theodosius was called *poenitentia publica* by Paulinus the Deacon (*Vita s. Ambrosii* 24 ML 14.35), by Augustine (*Serm.* 392.3 ML 39.1711), and by Rufinus (*Hist. eccl.* 2.18 ML 21.525). See Gal-

tier, *De poenitentia* 194, 195; Poschmann, *Augustini textus selecti de poenitentia* 6 n. 1.

188. In his *Speculum de Scriptura sacra* 29 CSEL 12.199 f., Augustine explicitly rejects the opinion that there are only three sins which are mortally sinful. Among those who were of this opinion was St. Pacian of Barcelona. Cf. *Paraenesis ad poenitentiam* 4, 5 ML 13.1083 f. See Durkin, *Theological Distinction of Sins* 18–21.

189. See nn. 43 and 45 above.

190. Matt. 13.25.

191. See Cyprian, *De lapsis* 5.6 CSEL 3.237 f. As a result of the edict of the Emperor Decius which was put in force at the end of the year 249 or at the beginning of 250, many Christians renounced their faith. These were the so-called *lapsi*, of which there were two categories: the *sacrificati*, who renounced their faith by an act of idolatry, and the *libellatici*, who secured for a sum of money certificates (*libelli*) attesting that they had actually renounced their faith, although they had not really done so. Even before the persecution was ended, some of the *lapsi* sought reinstatement in the Church. The greater part of them flocked to the confessors for permits of reconciliation which they might present to the priests. From the time of Tertullian, and perhaps even before that, it was admitted that those who suffered for the faith enjoyed a certain right to intercede on behalf of sinners. However, while some of the confessors were worthy of admiration, others were more or less trustworthy and of a doubtful prudence. These granted permits without requiring any guarantee of repentance or of doing penance.

In the letters written from his exile, Cyprian decided that when one who had fallen away had received a letter of reconciliation from a martyr and was in danger of death, it should be lawful to him to obtain peace by the ministry of a priest or, in case of necessity, of a simple deacon without waiting for the decision of the bishop. Cf. *Ep.* 18.1, 2 CSEL 3.523 f. He invited the confessors to abstain from abusing their privilege, reminding them that they had the right to recommend reconciliation but not the right to require or perform that reconciliation. Cf. *Ep.* 15.1; 16.1, 2; 17.1 CSEL 3.513 f., 517 f., 521 f. The views of Cyprian were solemnly sanctioned by the Council which met at Carthage in April 251, after the bishop's return. The

Council decided (1) that the letters of reconciliation granted by the martyrs would not be taken into account, and that the case of each of the *lapsi* would be examined individually; (2) that the *libellatici*, since they were less guilty, would be admitted to reconciliation after due enquiry; (3) the *sacrificati* were required to do penance all their life but would be reconciled at the time of death; (4) those *lapsi* who refused the *exhomologesis* could not be reconciled even *in articulo mortis*. Cf. Cyprian, *Ep.* 55.6, 13, 14, 17, 23 CSEL 3.627 ff., 635 ff. See de Labriolle, *History and Literature of Christianity* 147–53; Tixeront, *History of Dogmas* 1.346 ff.

192. Cf. Cyprian, *De lapsis* 5.6 CSEL 3.240 f.

193. Many of the Fathers condemn marriages between Catholics and pagans or heretics, without specifying, however, whether such marriages are null or only illicit. Cf. Tertullian, *Ad uxorem* 2.1–3 ML 1.1402–6; Cyprian, *De lapsis* 5.6 CSEL 3.240; Ambrose, *De Abraham* 1.9.84 ML 14.451; Jerome, *Adv. Jovinianum* 1.10 ML 23.234. But Augustine does not seem to share this opinion. He tells us here that in his time one no longer considered such marriages sinful. Although Jerome, a contemporary of Augustine, severely condemns this practice (*Adv. Jovinianum* 1.10 ML 23.223), Augustine is content to simply state the fact. He seems to say, in fact, that such marriages are not sinful. Since they are not clearly prohibited by Scripture, it is thought that they are permitted or, at least, it is doubted that they are sinful. He expresses the same thought in the *De conj. adult.* 1.25 CSEL 41.378. The obscurity of Scripture on this point and the custom of his time led Augustine to say that one no longer considered these marriages wrong. On the other hand, his doubts as to the meaning of St. Paul's doctrine in this matter (1 Cor. 7.39; 2 Cor. 6.14 ff.), and the fact that the rest of the Fathers thought other than he did, caused Augustine to be reserved in his opinion. This and the dire consequences involved in such marriages explain why, at the end of this chapter, he exhorts the faithful not to enter into such unions. It was these latter considerations especially which influenced Augustine to advise in one of his letters against the marriage of a certain Christian girl with a pagan. Cf. *Ep.* 255 CSEL 57.602. See Pereira, *La doctrine du mariage* 165–71.

194. Flavius Josephus mentions that Herod married his brother's wife while his brother was still living. Cf. *Antiquities of the Jews* 18.7.

195. Matt. 14.3 f.

196. As we already saw in n. 2 above, the Church was very careful not to admit to baptism anyone engaged in a profession or practice which was not compatible with the life required of a Christian, as, e.g., prostitutes, gladiators, etc. Certain cases, however, were more difficult to determine. The case referred to here is that of a concubine who is also the slave of a pagan master. She was admitted to baptism only on the condition that she broke off relations with her master, or married him legitimately, or she was allowed to remain with him in order to raise their children, provided she had relations only with him and no one else. See Bareille, "Catéchuménat" 2.2, 1972.

197. Cf. Matt. 5.32.

198. Augustine expresses a doubt here regarding the indissolubility of marriage. However, he gives his definitive doctrine in *De conjugiis adulterinis*, which he wrote six years later in 419. There he says that only death can break the bond (passim). The husband as well as the wife commits adultery in contracting another marriage. Cf. *De conj. adult.* 1.1; 2.9 CSEL 41.348, 391. The *nisi ex causa fornicationis* of Matt. 19.9 does not admit of any exception whatever. If our Lord speaks of an exception, it is only to point out the greater of two crimes. In other words, he who puts away his wife for no reason at all and marries another commits a greater sin of adultery than he who puts away his wife because of adultery and marries another. Moreover, the parallel texts in Mark 10.11 and Luke 16.18 mention no exceptions and they do not contradict Matthew. Cf. *De conj. adult.* 1.9; 1.11; 2.4 CSEL 41.355 f., 359 f., 386. See Ladomérszky, *Augustin, docteur du mariage* 104 ff., 146 ff. See n. 7 above.

199. See n. 87 above.

200. John 5.14.

201. Cf. Rom. 15.19.

202. Acts 2.40.

203. The baptism of John was a baptism of water and of penance for the remission of sins, but it was not John's baptism that remitted sin but the penance which accompanied it; hence Augustine calls it "remission of sins in hope." Cf. *De bapt.* 5.10, 12 ML 43.183.

Thomas Aquinas says that the baptism of John was not a sacrament of itself, but a certain sacramental, as it were, preparing the way for the baptism of Christ. Cf. *Sum. theol.* 3. q. 38, a. 1.

204. Cf. Luke 3.13.

205. Cf. James 2.19.

206. Gal. 5.6.

207. Luke 17.21.

208. Rom. 13.10.

209. Matt. 11.12.

210. Rom. 5.5.

211. John 17.3.

212. 1 John 2.3 f.

213. Matt. 22.40. For Augustine, charity is not only the principle of the moral life, it is the moral life. In *Enchiridion* 121 ML 41.288 he reduces all morality to charity: *omnis itaque praecepti finis est charitas, id est, ad charitatem refertur omne praeceptum.* In *De moribus ecclesiae* 1.15, 25 ML 32.1322 he regards all the virtues as various forms of charity. This is a fundamental idea of his which he states in various ways. Two loves, he says in the *City of God* 14.28 CSEL 40^2.56 f., built two cities: *fecerunt civitates duas amores duo: terrenam scilicet, amor sui usque ad contemptum Dei; coelestem vero amor Dei usque ad contemptum sui.* Yet charity does not destroy the virtues, but brings them to their full perfection. It does not suppress the precepts of the law, but unifies them and brings them to completion. Cf. *Enar. in ps.* 31.5 ML 36.260 f. See Portalié, "Augustin" 1.2.2435; Gilson, *Introduction* 182 ff.; Combes, *Oeuvres* 98 ff.

214. 1 John 3.23.

215. Ps. 41(40).5.

216. Wisd. 15.2.

217. Ibid.

218. Ibid.

219. According to Augustine, predestination is the eternal will of God which is realized, in some persons, in time; it is the act in virtue of which God determines those whom His mercy will take from the mass of sin and whom He will lead infallibly to eternal salvation. *Haec est praedestinatio sanctorum nihil aliud: praescientia scilicet et praeparatio beneficiorum Dei quibus certissime liberantur quicumque liberantur.* Cf. *De dono persev.* 14.35 ML 45.1014. Eternally in God, pre-

destination is realized in man in time. One in its cause, its execution is made up of several steps which are pointed out by St. Paul (Rom. 8.30). The first object of the divine will is the glory, the salvation, of those whom He has chosen. In order that they might attain this end, God confers on them successively the efficacious means: the graces of vocation, justification, and perseverance, all of which have the merits of Christ as their source. Cf. *De praed. sanct.* 17.34; 15.31 ML 44.983, 986.

The elect or predestined are those who are called according to the plan of God, *qui secundum propositum vocati sunt*, a terminology which Augustine takes from St. Paul and which he uses very often in his later works. It means that this calling is made in conformity with the decree deciding the salvation of those who are the object of this decree and who, consequently, cannot but respond to it. Cf. *Ep.* 186.7, 25 ML 33.825; *De praed. sanct.* 16.32 ML 44.983 and passim.

Predestination to the state of grace and eternal life, although related to the free will and merits of man, is nevertheless, in the last analysis, entirely dependent upon the infinitely free and merciful love of God. God, says Augustine, does not will the eternal salvation of man except as a crowning of his merits, but in crowning his merits He is only crowning His own gifts: *cum Deus coronat merita nostra, nihil aliud coronat quam munera sua* (*Ep.* 194.8 ML 33.874).

Augustine's thinking on predestination appears to some to be a kind of determinism. Cf. Rist, "Augustine on Free Will and Predestination" 218–52. But this is not the meaning of Augustine's teaching. He wrote his book *De gratia et libero arbitrio* to prove the freedom of the will. To do good, both grace and free will are necessary. Grace does not destroy the freedom of man; in fact, it helps his freedom: *neque enim voluntatis arbitrium ideo tollitur quia juvatur; sed ideo juvatur quia non tollitur.* Cf. *Ep.* 157.2, 10 ML 33.677.

Furthermore, Augustine does not teach a predestination to sin or hell. He rejects as blasphemy and as an impossibility the idea that God could predestine anyone to sin. God foresees the sin of the sinner and He permits it, but He does not will it nor does He cause it. Cf. *In Joan. tract.* 53.4 ML 30.1379.

The human mind is limited in its understanding of God and His ways. We must not, however, deny what is manifest because we do not know what is hidden. It is manifest that nothing regarding the elect is hidden to God. What is not manifest to us but hidden is the how and the why. Shall we say therefore, asks Augustine, that we do not know the manifest because we do not know the hidden, the how and the why? Cf. *De dono persev.* 14.37 ML 45.1016. See Jacquin, "La prédestination" 853–78; Chéné, *La théologie de saint Augustin* 74–82; Bernard, "La prédestination" 4–7.

220. 1 John 2.1 f.

221. Rom. 2.12.

222. John 5.28 f.

223. Gal. 5.6.

224. In Augustine's time the dogma of the resurrection was violently attacked by the pagans. See *Enar. in ps.* 88.5 ML 37.1134. Augustine answers all their objections in *De civ. Dei* 22.12–20 CSEL 40^2. 618–34, and in *Serm.* 361 ML 39.1599 f. See Arand, ACW 3.137 n. 287.

225. John 3.18.

226. Rom. 2.12.

227. Rom. 4.15.

228. Rom. 7.7.

229. Rom. 5.5.

230. Rom. 2.12.

231. In saying that it is more serious to sin when one has knowledge of the law than when one is ignorant of the law, Augustine shows that ignorance diminishes the guilt of sin but not that it excuses one entirely. He states many times that ignorance of the law, even involuntary ignorance, does not excuse one from sin, since ignorance and error are consequences of original sin. Infidels, e.g., are not saved if they are ignorant of the truth; their punishment can only be diminished. Cf. *De gratia et lib. arb.* 3.5 ML 44.884 f. Concerning ignorance as a punishment of sin, see Martin, *Saint Augustin* 211–18.

232. Rom. 2.12.

233. This paragraph belongs to chapter 23.

234. Gal. 4.31.

235. Gal. 5, 13.

236. 1 Peter 2.16.

237. 2 Peter 2.17–22.

238. 2 Peter 2.21.

239. Gal. 5.6.

240. 2 Peter 2.20.
241. 2 Peter 2.13.
242. Jude 1.12.
243. Cf. James 2.20.
244. Matt. 12.45.
245. Cf. Gen. 19.26.
246. 1 Tim. 1.13.
247. Matt. 23.15.
248. Augustine shows here that baptism is absolutely necessary for salvation. However, he recognized substitutes for the sacrament, e.g. martyrdom, or faith and conversion of heart, if it is impossible to receive the sacrament. Cf. *De pec. mer. et remis.* 1.23 ML 44, 128; *Enchir.* 13.43 ML 40.253; *De bapt.* 4.29 ML 43.173; *Cont. litt. Petil.* 2.52 ML 43.276.
249. John 3.5.
250. Matt. 5.20.
251. Matt. 23.2 f.
252. See nn. 185, 186 above.
253. 1 Cor. 5.4 f.
254. 2 Cor. 12.21.
255. See n. 187 above.
256. The words of Augustine are: *nisi essent quaedam non ea humilitate poenitentiae sananda . . . sed quibusdam correptionum medicamentis.* The meaning of these words is a subject of controversy. Some hold that Augustine is speaking here of private confession for certain less serious sins which might be called intermediary, i.e. between the greater serious sins which must be atoned for by public penance and the little sins which can be forgiven by prayer; that he is distinguishing here in this whole passage between three classes of sins and three kinds of remedies proper to each class. The remedy for the intermediary sins is the *correptio,* i.e. a secret or private correction and pardon between the priest and the sinner. Others, on the contrary, understand these words to mean simply a reproof or an exhortation to do penance. This reproof or exhortation is concerned only with certain species of sins and may be made publicly, as in sermons, or in private either by a priest or by anyone of the faithful. Its purpose is to induce the sinner to repent and thus in this sense it may be called a remedy for sin. See Galtier, *De poenitentia* 326 ff.; Adam, *Die geheime*

Kirchenbusse 39 ff.; Poschmann, *Kirchenbusse* 44 ff. See also Palmer, "Jean Morin," *Theol. Studies* 6 (1945) 317–57; 7 (1946) 281–308; La Bonnardière, "Pénitence" 1.279–82; Durkin, *Theological Distinction of Sins* 41 ff.; Mortimer, *Origins of Private Penance* 68–74, 102–10; Kelly, *Early Christian Doctrines* 438–40.

257. Matt. 18.15.

258. This petition of the Lord's Prayer is Augustine's favorite answer to those who say that it is possible to live without sin in this life. The Pelagians believed and taught that a person who knew the commandments of God could attain perfection of sanctity in this life without the grace of God and by his own free will. Consequently, it was not necessary for such a person to say "forgive us our debts." In 418 Augustine wrote to Count Boniface (*Ep.* 189.8 CSEL 57.136): "Never imagine that you are without sin, no matter how much progress you have made in love of God and your neighbor, and in true religion. . . . As long as you are in the body, you must say, 'Forgive us our debts, as we forgive our debtors.' " There is no verse of the Our Father that Augustine develops more than this one. And there is no thought that recurs more often in his writings. For some examples see *De civ. Dei* 19.27; 22.23 CSEL 40^2.422, 641; *De continentia* 11.25 CSEL 41.173; *De sancta virginitate* 48 CSEL 41.294; *De pec. mer. et remis.* 2.16, 24 ML 44.166; *Serm.* 56.8–12 ML 38.382. See Moffatt, "Augustine on the Lord's Prayer" 259–72; La Bonnardière, "Les commentaires" 131 ff., 141 ff.; Hamman, "Le Nôtre Père" 57 ff.

259. Prov. 31.27.

260. Scripture here = *divinum eloquium.* The Fathers often use *eloquium* (="diction") to mean Holy Scripture itself. See Christopher, ACW 2.112 n. 97; Arand, ACW 3.117 n. 17.

261. Matt. 19.17.

262. Cf. Matt. 19.18.

263. Cf. James 2.20.

264. Gal. 5.6.

265. Cf. Cyprian, *De lapsis* 27 CSEL 3.256 f.

INDEXES

1. OLD AND NEW TESTAMENT

2. AUTHORS AND SOURCES

3. LATIN WORDS

4. GENERAL INDEX